"*Archipelago in a Landlocke[...]* documenting place as chara[...] through a magnifying lens made oi stained glass. Patient and meditative, acute and animate, aromatic and auditory—this is a captivating, nearly mythological work of tableau and vignette in the shape of a pilgrimage. A threshold into a new way of writing."

Sarah Gerard, author of *True Love*

"Elisa Taber writes with the economy of a poet, the precision of a translator, and the imagination of a novelist, bringing a sharp ethnographic eye to her singular descriptions of Paraguay. Original, arresting, and strikingly cinematic, *An Archipelago in a Landlocked Country* is a compelling text— experimental yet accessible, challenging yet thoroughly satisfying."

Hugh Raffles, author of *The Book of Unconformities*

"*An Archipelago in a Landlocked Country* offers a unique three-part journey deep into the heart of Paraguay. The Mennonite colony where the author was born and its neighbouring Indigenous community provide the background and inspiration for a filmic travelogue, a collection of short stories, and a novella. Taber is an astute observer, able to capture minute and surprising details while maintaining a deep respect for her characters, a personal appreciation for their histories and mythologies, and a gift for crafting wise contemporary fables. Her poetic sensibility and disarmingly precise prose combine to propel this vivid exploration of an existing territory as re-imagined in the present and into the future."

Joseph Schreiber, *3:AM Magazine*

"A birth tree, worn sneakers, blood and ocean. Taber's field writings are delicately precise, carefully tracing the speculative life of a third generation Mennonite woman."

Maria Fusco, author of *Legend of the Necessary Dreamer*

"This is a book of exceedingly thick description, by turns memoir, parable, sociological study, dirge. A self-professed "foreigner," Taber travels to the place of her birth, a Mennonite colony. Here, as she attempts to see, she discovers a series of insoluble blindspots, in the process bringing to light questions about what language or poetry could be adequate to a site she hopes to witness but to which she can never fully return."

Lucy Ives, author of *Loudermilk*

"*An Archipelago in a Landlocked Country* is consumed with looking and as such, offers a style of seeing so obsessed, so careful, and so meticulously considered that it borders on devotional. Taber's world is occupied by those who "wish the air was thicker and less translucent. Not to impede sight and movement but to render it visible." Relentlessly, we are reminded that to gaze and to be gazed upon is to be bound up, inextricably, in the web of memory, imagination, boundaries, and bodies."

**Candice Wuehle, author of *Bound* and
*Death Industrial Complex***

"A stunningly poetic triptych, arresting in its mastery, told in spare yet rich, affecting style, *An Archipelago in a Landlocked Country* is utterly transportive. Taber's lyric tapestry transports the reader to starkly contrasting worlds within a singular region, of Paraguay and the human heart. Laced together, every microscopic detail adds a strand to a larger, sweeping portrait of utterly absorbing people, places, and journeys we are fortunate Taber allows us to encounter."

Liza Monroy, author of *Mexican High* and *The Marriage Act*

AN ARCHIPELAGO IN A LANDLOCKED COUNTRY

Requests for permission should be directed to 1111@1111press.com, or mailed to 11:11 Press LLC, 4732 13th Ave S., Minneapolis, MN 55407.

Cover photograph: "Vista dall' alto del cerro. Puerto Casado-Puerto Celina" by Guido Boggiani. Ca 1896. Reproduced in GUIDO BOGGIANI, PHOTOGRAPHER, by Pavel Frič and Yvonna Fričová, Ed. Titanic, Prague, 1997. Courtesy Yvonna Fričová.

Page & Cover Design: Tyler Crumrine

Library of Congress Control Number: 2019948636

eBook: 9781948687133
Paperback: 9781948687126

Printed in the United States of America

FIRST AMERICAN EDITION

9 8 7 6 5 4 3 2 1

AN ARCHIPELAGO IN A LANDLOCKED COUNTRY

A LYRIC ETHNOGRAPHY
BY ELISA TABER

Introduction   1

I.   **Asunción to Neuland, via Filadelfia**   3

    a.   Asunción   4

    b.   Filadelfia   18

    c.   Neuland   38

II.   **Cayim ô Clim**   49

    a.   A Bracelet   50

    b.   Raising Angel   53

    c.   Sombra Is a Horse   59

    d.   The Match   62

    e.   Not Sinking but Floating   71

    f.   Holding Hands   80

    g.   Holding Her Hand   82

    h.   A Rock Like a Drop of Water   87

    i.   Birds Plead When They Sing   92

    j.   The Face of a Dove   106

    k.   Tiny Tombstones   109

III. La Paz del Chaco Street   121

  a. Agatha   122

    i. Estela   122

    ii. Karin   125

    iii. The Cattle Driver   130

    iv. Greta   151

      1. A Painting   155

      2. A Sermon   157

    i. Tanuuj   163

      3. A Statue   170

    i. Karin   179

    ii. Verena   181

      4. A Home   187

  a. Concepción   192

Para mi madre, que me contaba cuentos.

The indigenous people who call themselves Nivaklé live in the Gran Chaco. They are nomads that remained voluntarily isolated for nearly three hundred years after the Spanish conquest of Paraguay. Following the War of the Triple Alliance and the Chaco War, the national government scrambled to populate the unclaimed region. Canadian Mennonites purchased the extent of land where the Enlhet, Ayoreo, and Nivaklé had been living since the previous century. There they established two colonies: Menno, in 1927, and Fernheim, in 1930. Refugees fleeing persecution in Soviet Russia founded a third, Neuland, in 1947. It was known as Frauendorf, the women's village, as all one hundred forty-seven of the adult inhabitants were female. No longer subsisting off Menno and Fernheim charity, they became not settlers, but pioneers.

I was conceived in Neuland in 1990. I do not remember the bush Frieda planted when I was conceived, or the peach tinged roses I received when I was born. I remember Dolores Ayerza's *Reserva Campo Alegre*, my mother's painting. The baby in the forefront and the title scrawled at the bottom. He is limp but rigid in his mother's arms. Her lips and nose are swollen but severe. In the background there is a man with mouth agape, a squalid dog, and a wooden chair. When I was older, I was told the baby was dead. In January 2013, I returned to Neuland on my own. I lived with Frieda Müller for three months. She is a self-described Mennonite and Chaqueña. In July 2016, my mother and I return together to Frieda's unoccupied home for a month.

We break the trip into three legs. Two hours by plane from Buenos Aires to Asunción. I see the cluster of colonies through a small oval window. In a sea of brown, a green kidney shaped stain delineated in red. The line demarcates the laborers' camps. Eight hours by bus from Asunción to Filadelfia, a town in the Fernheim Colony and the capital of the Boquerón Department. The headrest cocoons mother's deaf ear. Vestibular nerves, like braided fibers, grow worn and unravel. The heavy object they are tethered to falls into a vacuum. That is the hollowness that resounds within. One hour by car from Filadelfia to Neuland. The drone of the engine fills the cavity and subsumes her tinnitus. The main avenue stretches from the *quebracho* monument that marks the entrance into the colony to the fiftieth anniversary monument that signals the exit onto the Transchaco Highway. Cross the latter to reach Cayim ô Clim, the Nivaklé settlement. Turn left on La Perdiz, left onto La Paz del Chaco, and right into Frieda's rose bush lined driveway. The silent house empties the filled cavity and now it is my mother who is subsumed. That night I dream of being underwater. Hear the waves crash. It is the droning wind.

I.

Asunción to Neuland, via Filadelfia

Asunción

A slim window lines a wall of the stairwell. From the fifth-floor landing the city is in bloom. Patches of pink stain the streets that descend towards the river. This year the *lapachos* are early. A month or so. After the rain their petals litter the floor. Trampled into clumps barely protruding above the smooth pavement. The tree that was in bloom the day I was born.

Peering over Ofelia's balcony, I remember wanting to name a daughter after her. She used to live in a house built around a pool. I swam there alone. Her German shepherd encircled me. I laid my forearms on the rim. He knelt before me, his lips curled, and teeth showed. Neither of us made a sound. Her hand materialized on the crown of his head, gently stroking. I safely lifted myself up and out. My sisters and I assumed she would care for us, if our parents died.

Her plastic enveloped mattress propped against the metal fence is being aired. Where the sheath sticks, because it is moist, the pattern grows visible. A flower so meaty that the petals peel back and the tips hang heavy. I steer the flip camera to the upper right corner. There, dangles a small garment. It is the discolored shade of black that cloth lathered and rinsed too many times acquires.

My mother chokes. Turns to the window. I stand on the opposite side. "Cough with your mouth closed," Ofelia instructs. Her cheeks and jowl tremble. Their voices grow muffled by a hammerhead. It is breaking through the wall between the *lomitería* and the apartment complex. Then, a sequence of cars. They run parallel to me. I hear them approach through my left ear and see them pass. "You're at home," someone says. I am not sure who or to whom.

A woman stands at the door of the building at street level. It is Alfonsina. The bell rings within. Her eyes caress the outline of my face. Then, rise to the sky. A thread woven through the eye of her needle stitches me to her. When the medicine wears off, she sees through me. She would have frightened me when I was younger. With age madness has become less threatening. It has for her ex-husband too. After he institutionalized her, he married a younger woman. There is a fragility to her now.

The three sixty-year-old women and I settle around the dining table.

Dolores recounts her sister's phobia: Inocencia believed her eyes rolled in their sockets while she slept. My great-grandmother, Mariquita, tied a ribbon over her lids every night to hold them in place. It is an anecdote. We laugh. I love mother most of all.

Alfonsina says she feels sand on her corneas. The grains scratch her lids when she closes them. She tries to keep them open. They become so dry the itch is as painful as the tear.

The dreams they retell grow increasingly vivid.

Ofelia traces the scar on her throat with her index while she speaks. The silk scarf around her neck gapes. It is as though the nail wants to indent and rip the suture. I want to tell her she looks beautiful.

I grow languorous before speaking. Distance myself instead. Move to the couch. Watch the white Persian cat. A bowl of silicone teeth on the coffee table. It tumbles the molds onto the beige carpet. They meld. It nibbles on a canine. My body becomes heavy. I close my eyes. Sleep.

Dream. Christ on the cross. All I see are his feet. Where the spike nails flesh to wood, drops of blood seep.

Wake. Alone. A white sheet draped over me. It is five in the morning. I fainted, from heat exhaustion. Sweat makes my bare arms and legs adhere to the black leather.

We leave Asunción this morning, I remember.

Retiro is the name of the bus terminal. It means retreat, not from confrontation. The act of pulling away. Ofelia drives into the parking lot. Nuestra Señora de la Asunción is the bus service from Asunción to Buenos Aires. It backs out, turns right, and up the ramp.

I drag my bag across the floor of the empty basement. Access to the street is faster above, in the waiting area. Easier for someone to rip the bag off your shoulder. Watch them disappear between the columns that hold up the ceiling of the wall-less structure which houses vehicles and the passengers within them.

A white sheet is draped over the cold tiled floor. Purple and yellow, red and green, and turquoise and black woven bracelets; dog tags strung to metal drain stopper chains; and rosaries so long you can wear them crossbody like sashes.

Alongside the trinkets, a baby. She lies on her back atop a disassembled cardboard box. Short arms spread above her head. Hands nearly touching. Legs tilted left so her torso twists. She cannot be comfortable. Still she sleeps. A green, purple, pink, and yellow netted blanket neither keeps her warm nor conceals her lower half.

The mother suckles a spoonful of ice cream. A tub at her feet. Two large spoons, one plastic and one steel, buried in it. Her free hand gestures at the items for sale. Then, caresses her neck. A dollop of strawberry drips onto her lap. The rest makes it into her still open mouth. Her gums are so swollen. They are redder than the cream and occlude the teeth she has left.

At the top of the staircase there is a large figure on a tall but frail stool. Her proportionally little feet do not reach the ground. Where her bum meets the flat surface, plump but hardened flanks bulge. The starched cotton of her white apron caresses but does not curve with her flesh. Her invisible hands, turned fists, burrow into her sides.

"*Chipá, chipita, chipita, chipá,*" she cries out. Her voice resonates on the last vowel—ah. Plastic, wrapping a pile of five or six dense yucca and cheese wheels, gleams. White, rather than translucent, are the lines where the material wrinkles and protrudes. Passing torsos and thighs obstruct my view of the saleswoman.

She turns to one side, the other, and then, towards me. Raises her eyebrows and purses her lips. When the film grows focused her expression disappears. Her sign is illegible. "624" is hand painted on the wall behind her. Perhaps the number means something or nothing at all.

A mother and two adolescent daughters sit before a row of buses. They are blond. I assume they are Mennonites. Ask them if the one with the hummingbird plastered on its side goes to Neuland. They seem to know and nod. The eldest stands apart from her family and lights a cigarette. She smokes and pretends not to see everyone stare.

We return at the time of departure. Mother and a daughter are gone. The girl is alone and younger than I am. The resemblance between us surprises and then, humiliates me. At twenty-three, I *was* her. I traveled to Neuland alone. I read the Nivaklé's erotic myths on the bus. I was unaware of how my presence provoked.

There is a lion on her sweatshirt. She wears it despite the heat.

A boy sits between his mother and younger sister. He takes a syringe and a small glass vessel from a cooler. The plastic vessel fills with the clear liquid. He does not prick his elbow pit. Instead, pulls his shirt up. Pinches his abdomen. Pierces the soft skin. Injects the insulin. Looks up. Neither grimaces nor smiles. Just sees me. Then, closes his eyes.

We board the NASA Picaflor, the bus from Asunción to Filadelfia. I do not know what the acronym means. A bird resembling the illustration on the bus hovers above Alfonsina's head. She waves from the platform. I remember her mouthing, "Welcome." When Ofelia and Alfonsina see me, they only see twenty-five years. Time materialized in the aging of a human body.

Mother is always by the window.

The driver's compartment draws open. His substitute sits on the steps to the door. The sign on it does not read "*tirar*" (pull) but "*estirar*" (stretch). Beside him a large thermos. He turns the knob and tilts it. Cold water pours into the *guampa*. It is made of a cattle horn. Tin, not silver, encircles the rim. He sips and passes the *tereré*. A DIY cupholder encased in the window frame protrudes from the skeleton of the car, like an arm. After four hours they trade seats. The conductor becomes the companion.

A couple occupies the two seats across the aisle from us. His head is on her lap. Her body is upright. Her gaze is set on the sliver of road visible above the headrest. We are always at the broadest width. Ahead and behind us it is endlessly narrower. The boy is already asleep. Long, greasy strands of hair spread over the large yellow and red flowers on her skirt. She combs his hair with her fingers. He turns to face her. Pus-filled pimples on his cheek.

A stand by the side of the road sells toy ducks. Sticks attached to their spines. Wheels under their bums. The girl that sells them demonstrates. Grabs hold of a pole. Pushes. Its feet swing round. Inanimate simulations of will puncture my faith. The sun strikes their small heads. Their features are blurred in the low resolution of my camera screen. A yellow or pink helium balloon tied to each. Thirty of them in a row form a barrier between the highway and abandoned lot, unless driven over by a passing motorbike, car, or truck.

The bus starts and stops to pick up passengers and travelling salesmen. One sells flashlights, clipped to keychains attached to his belt loops; and watches, clasped to his wrists and forearms. He flips a lantern on and off by rubbing his thumb over the two silicone lined buttons.

Another offers vegetable sandwiches. Chopped hardboiled eggs and mayonnaise between the first two layers of wonder bread. Two thin slices of tomato and margarine between the second.

The last peddles ointments. He speaks in Guaraní. Potential customers inspect the merchandise but do not purchase. I pick up a large beige tub. "*Grasa de Mula*" (Mule Fat) is the name on the label. An illustration of the heavy headed animal. And the warning, "*Para uso externo. Correr.*" (For External Use. Run.) I assume, rub. In the Neuland co-op a sticker covers the list of ingredients. It reads, "*Dios te ama.*" (God loves you.) Below, in smaller type, "*Gott liebt dich.*"

Traffic stalls as we turn off the road. Up a ramp to the highway. It encircles a *lapacho*. The branches hover over me. Frail blooms dangle weightlessly from their twigs. The first is dark. The latter, sparse and shriveled. It rained last night. Between them the light shines through.

Aiming the camera up. Blinded when the tree does not block the sun. Behind it is a staircase leading to the highway. Driving up the slope I look to my left. From above it provides a shelter below. Flowers clump together covering branches. Parts conform a whole.

A pair of legs between a turquoise trashcan and a yellow wall. The bus pulls away.

The road leading to the Transchaco Highway weaves through the outskirts. We trace a semicircle around a roundabout. The driver steers left. Heavy heads on loose necks tilt right. We stop to watch a pedestrian trace a diagonal through the center.

Behind the bus stop, a wall. Scrawled on it, *"Soy infeliz."* (I am unhappy.) A wire dangles from the rim. One end is creviced between bricks. The other, wrapped around a wooden stick. The handles of a plastic bag are woven through the pole. I film the bag sway with the gust of wind of a passing car. In the twenty-second video I see a bird fly past the same wall. The shadow is only visible in movement, invisible in a film still. I must press play.

A yellow stripe streams crosswise through a red square on the floor. The latter marks the entrance to a building and the first limits where a car may park. Loud inhale. "Even better" is uttered loudly. A man in a red shirt and pale skin, glistening with sweat, walks past.

I guess the words on the wall say, "'*Liberen a Rubén vivo.*' —*La JP*" ("Free Ruben alive." —The JP\). The "P" has sprouted a leg. A can before it. Lift it. One end of a fishing line is attached to the can. The opposite end is buried deep between two tiles. One is loose. Lift it. Pull on the line. A cockroach emerges from the soil. Its wafer-thin wing pierced by the fishing hook.

Cacti strive to grow at the foot of the wall where the plaster has chipped off. A steel-toe shoe kicked until it exposed brick. It was the pain in his gut that shot his foot into the wall until his toes bled and he fell to his knees.

The wall, tiles, can, and cockroach stand before a tree. It casts a faint shadow but does not enter the frame. Its leaves rustle. Light flickers between them. Gusts of wind will shake them free. The trunk will remain. Black when moistened by the rain and gray when withered by the sun.

The traffic barrier casts a shadow to the right. It indicates that the sun behind me peers over my left shoulder. The orange head of the traffic cone points to the mound of red and yellow cautionary tape. Nestled together they are pink. All are mud splattered.

Tire marks on the now dry patch of dirt. A puddle remains by the barrier. The water is shaped like an oval. Rewind.

A child with a full bucket. His name is Juan. Turns with arms outstretched until the rim faces him. The liquid pours out all at once. It splashes his filthy jeans and the tips of his shoes. He feels tall, fast, and invisible, not invincible.

His mother calls out to him from their front yard. She knows that he wanders into the construction site in disuse. Where abandoned materials are "stored." He climbs atop the barrier. Like a gymnast traces the length without falling. The soles of his worn sneakers feel the narrow width of the pole. Such pride when he turns on his toes to face the opposite way and unmounts.

He tears the construction tape from the utility pole. Grabs one end and runs from one pole to the next. His speed, not strength, tears adhesive from cement. Gathers the tape into a large clump under his bicep. The mound falls softly, making as little noise as the pat pat of his feet.

The *sopa paraguaya*, corn meal baked dry, fills his open mouth. It soaks his saliva like a clump of quenched earth. Flour and dirt, petals and lettuce leaves, and soda and muddy water. The bus roars past. He has grown used to the sound of traffic. It provides constancy. A low wall of interwoven thorn branched trees conceals his home. No need for him to look up to see me.

A stain on the glass picks at the landscape. Its beak is narrow. It is closed. It swallows but cannot digest. Its neck is broad. It does not join body (missing) to head (faceless). The bird is absent.

The icing on someone's thumb left a translucent smudge. Stroke it. Feel the crevices on the fingerprint. It was moist before it dried, white.

A child handled a pastry. Saw something. Stood on his mother's thighs. Poised both hands on the window. His finger slid and left this mark.

Look past it. Rough, yellow grass and green palm trees. Tall blades and long, slim leaves. Not the trunks. They are burnt black. Let us call them stems. Plains are lit. Fires are contained. Crops and grass grow back. The trees remain. They are rooted deeper in soil.

Everything turns blue; then, green; then, white. Landscape and stain expunged by stripes on a passing truck. Across the tank, "*Gas Licuado de Petróleo*" (Liquefied Petroleum Gas). It runs opposite our bus. Legible when I drag my cursor back. Right to left. Find a rhombus. A line traced between a red "1" and a yellow "4." Another between the yellow "4" and a green "O." They constitute the triangular tip of the diamond.

A gap where truck bed and driver's compartment meet. Numerous palms sprout in the interstice. The truck disappears.

There is nothing to see. A single *palo santo* tree. So close to the road. Forefront to the background that remains the same. Branches curve in and sprout up, as in pain. Its patches of leaves resemble moss. Almost phosphorescent on the stone surface. When lit, the wood exudes a scent. It is sold as incense.

Frieda's husband carved and polished the lumber. Spheres line her shelves. Soft when stroked. Impenetrable if poked. Lift one. It weighs heavy on your palm. At chest height I smell it. Bring it close. Pungent like sweat but sweet enough to linger in the air and your memory.

You remember the smell of smoke or urine when it is gone.

Pozo Colorado is a border town in the Presidente Hayes Department, close to the Boquerón Department. Pass the military base when you enter. A large roundabout where the Transchaco and Coronel Franco highways intersect. When you exit pass the gas station.

In the middle of the grassy traffic circle there is a sculpture. Blue tires piled so high I have to slide down my pleather seat to see the tip. A couple at the foot of the statue. She sits to his left. Her head rests on his right leg. Her fingers interlock behind his neck. He peers down. Their gazes meet at a distance. Clenching his spine holds both of them in place.

A sign composed of potted flowers and tinted grass. It marks the entrance of Coronel Valois Rivarola, the military base. The trunks of all the trees are painted white up to the same height. Long, two-story buildings stretch behind them. Before one, a round picnic table with an umbrella poking out of the hole in the center. Beside it, a running track with hurdles in a row. The cuffs of their wooden legs match the trees.

We pull into the gas station. The fluorescent light of the overhead metal canopy is otherworldly. Metal and plastic grow pristine when the fluorescent light shines on its curves making them gleam. Despite the pretense it has a dirt floor. Behind it, a convenience store. A banner hangs above the entrance: "El Rapidito." Men wearing orange vests lounge on the curb in front of the automatic doors. When their arms spread to gesture, they slide open.

A soldier with black shoes and belt, buckled tight, hands me a bundle of keys. The smallest opens the bathroom padlock. I wait outside for my mother. My second cousin, Pelayo, had to stand guard with a loaded gun by his parents' locked bedroom while they napped. They lived on a farm in Entre Ríos. No one but them for a twenty-kilometer circumference. The door before me is closed. Light still streams through the three seams. Where it screws to the frame only the hinges glisten. I turn. Behind a metal fence and a deep ditch, a field of tall grass. That is what I see in the dark.

We board. I realize my shoes and socks are red with dirt. The driver turned companion walks to the rear. Row by row he offers a small glass full of orange soda. Most of the passengers have fallen asleep. Only a toddler sitting between the laps of his mother and aunt is rustling awake. He turns onto his back to face them. With eyes closed one raises a soft hand to pat him on the back. He whines a little. It is barely audible.

I grow aware of the soundtrack of a film blasting through the speakers. It is not the sound of artillery or cries for help that disturb my mother, but the hero's screeching commands. She has always been disobedient.

It is pitch-black outside. No high-mast poles hovering over the highway, windows of homes lit within, or fires burning in front gardens. Only palm trees with the foot of each trunk burnt black in an interminable plane of tall grass.

There is light within. The small screens that protrude from the ceiling emit it. During the second half of the trip I watch *Olympus Has Fallen* and the sequel, *London Has Fallen*. Bring my legs to my chest and the soles of my feet to the pleather of the seat.

Four hours later the illusion of comfort vanishes. The landscape has changed. The night cloaks an impenetrable net of trees, lianas, and bushes. All the plants have thorns. Even the maternally bloated *palo borracho* has spines on its trunk.

I can tell we are approaching Filadelfia because streetlights appear and disappear at an intermittent rate. The first emits a faint, green glow on a mound of dirt. Maybe there is a little city below. An ant colony. Tunnels leading to chambers. Here they sleep. There, lay eggs. Here, hatch. There, store food. A patch of grass by the entry. The camera flashes red in the reflection. It accompanies the streetlight like a firefly. Light blurs as the bus speeds.

Then, stalls again. The silhouette of a house. Light emanates from its windows. Slabs of cardboard substitute blinds. One slaps open and closed. Someone is asleep on a cot inside. A nude fleece blanket covers the stone body. His feet slip out from under it. A rim of long, dark hairs around his ankles. Red pimples erupt below the human pelt. He turns away from me on his side.

Except for the adolescent and the infant, all the passengers are asleep. The teenager's brown skin has acquired a sickly tinge, yellow. He is the one that injected insulin. Neck arches. Crown touches nape. Eyelids flutter closed. In his sleep night materializes. He draws close to the darkness transformed into a wall. Touches it with the tips of his toes, chest, and nose. Chin to chest. Forehead presses in until dust-laden lashes caress the cement. Something seeps between his legs. Fear is not audible in dreams.

I fall asleep. My nose is bleeding. The gentle seeping makes my head grow buoyant though encased in its skull.

The second streetlight has a warm yellow tint. A wisp of a bush. Behind it a short but entrenched forest. Lianas and plants with thorns. Fall to your knees to crawl. The needles will prick your skin. See the mound of flesh by the side of the road? Oh, its beautiful, wet mane. Beside it, a puddle of blood. Behind it, a tunnel. A boar's skin is thick. If punctured, it still bleeds. It stampeded rather than crept through the tunnel. Such force leads to exhaustion. A pulsing body inhales frigid air. An unstoppable body does not curl up to recuperate. After a feat of strength, it falls. Expects to be trampled.

The third is a lit sign. In the colonies, signage is in English, Spanish, and German, not Guaraní. A roll encased in a window frame runs around slowly enough for you to read.

How to make your son a delinquent:

1. Give him money. He will not suspect you work for it.

2. Tell him he is right. He will think those who punish him want to harm him.

3. Fight with your partner. He will not think your family is dysfunctional. He will destroy his own.

This is Filadelfia. The expanse between one structure and the next collapses. Space becomes clearly delineated by streets that intersect one another and separate one block from the next. Silhouettes of larger, more concrete, homes, office buildings, and stores. The colony appears empty. It is cold.

In Asunción people sit outdoors at night. It is always warm. Some on lawn chairs and others on stiff wooden chairs with desks attached. The women roll up the cuffs of their leggings over their knees to scratch their calves. Even knee creases exude droplets of sweat. They stream down to ankles, over flip flops, onto the dry soil. Children dig into it with their plastic shovels. They dig holes that fill when it rains. When it ceases, they make paper boats that float in them. The youngest dunks her feet in. The boats flood, paper dampens, grows formless, heavy, and sinks.

There is no music. Not even the booming voice of Padre Pedro streaming softly from a neighboring radio. The attendant hovers over me. It is ten at night. He does not say a word. We pick up the bags held in place between our feet. I put on my backpack. Take one strap of my mother's duffle. We walk diagonally to the front. The bus door folds open. Before we descend the assistant asks: "You stay here?" I feel the nudge of his palm against the place where my back curves. I am a prisoner on a plank. He hurls me into an unknowable depth. It is just dark.

I hear two pairs of feet land after mine. First, my mother. Then, the adolescent Mennonite girl.

Filadelfia

We stand on a patch of grass encased between the dirt road and the paved sidewalk. I see the outline of a one-story brick building. I run my hand along the back of the bumpers of the trucks parked in line in the lot. A planter with a bush inside marks the entrance. We encircle it and the automatic doors slide open. Behind the clerk an enlarged satellite image of the hotel. On the top right corner, "Hotel Florida" in comic sans beside a cartoon of an *ombú*.

Four walls enclose two perpendicular buildings that meet to create a right angle. One is the sleeping quarters. The other, the lobby and restaurant. A grass plot encircles a cement platform. A tiny *ombú* at the center. Root barriers below ground disable it from wrapping around pipelines or raising the bases of the neighboring edifices. A turquoise rectangle behind the lawn, a pool. The color of the tiles is visible through the translucent water. The light bulb on the ceiling casts a reflection where the adjacent block starts.

Walk to the counter to take a closer look. The clerk peers up and sets my key down with a soft thud. The hallway rims the courtyard to my left. Even in the dark I see the tree in the paved square, the garden pathway rimmed in bushes of flowers, and the otherworldly glow of the lights along the sides of the pool. The guestrooms to my right. Each has a window the width of a wall. They are tinted black. The plastic trash can, brick column, and tiled floor reflect on the glass turned mirror. If you squint all you see are its metallic tones and the folds of the heavy curtain within.

The guestroom matches the size of the dining hall. Two king sized beds. A flat screen television hung on the opposite wall. An air conditioner humming as it cools. Two double-doored floor-to-ceiling wardrobes. Still the room feels empty. First, the floor is swept; the spaces between the beige tiles are scrubbed; then, it is mopped. I carried dirt on the soles of my shoes. Gusts of wind sweep more under the door. No one walks outdoors. There are southern winds. Tiny grains hoist themselves off the ground in waves. They prick your forehead, cheeks, and the bridge of your nose like ice pellets.

There are two locks on the interior side of the bathroom door. Three frosted glass panes encircle the shower. Above it, a narrow window. Wide enough to peer through. Not just an opening that exhausts steam to prevent mold growth. Wrap opposite ends of a hand towel around screws nailed to the top corners of the frame. It drapes over the glass. The chamber fills with steam. Enclosed by three walls and a sliding door. Where the towel droops I peer out onto a leafy canopy. The sleeping quarters are built on an elevated platform so no one of average height on the other side of the wall can reach the window and peer in at the guests.

Sitting on the bed in my towel I notice the showcase compartment above the wardrobe. The furniture is too large, clunky. Many pieces have hidden compartments. I wonder what I can stash in them and if anyone will know to look. Some are not built to occlude but serve an odd, practical purpose. A closet between two rooms can be opened from either side. Turn the switch on the right wall of the cupboard.

Two vessels encased in pine and glass. Each in the center of its respective shelf. A spotlight above each turns on. They cast a faint shadow on the wood's growth rings. Glazed brown jars glisten where they curve.

Their presence in a room implies that the couple that inhabits it seeks to conceive. They are fertility jugs. Modeled after a woman's waist or a baby's neck. Wring the child's neck like I did my underwear in the sink.

The mouth of the vase is wide. Standing on a chair I take one off the shelf. Grasp it where the rim curves in. Peer into the contents. Like the secret drawers and compartments, it is empty. *El fondo* means the bottom but also what is left. The mix of saliva and coke in your nearly empty bottle.

They are made of clay collected from the Pilcomayo river. I imagine muddy water, like a mirror reflecting the sun's beams. A slimy eel slithers along the floor and coils around my ankles. I cannot take another step. Soil crevices under my nails. Something distracting. It slithers away. I do not move for a clear and mistaken reason, fear.

A constant, low hum. It may be the cooling system or one of the light bulbs. Before my mother steps out of the bathroom, I turn them off. Standing in the dark I listen and try to situate myself in relation to the furnishings. My bed and the one adjacent are to my left, the two wardrobes are to my right, the suitcases by the door are behind me, and the flickering light of the heater is before me. I am forgetting something. Turn the light back on. Everything is as it was.

With the curtains drawn and all the doors locked, I feel the way I did in the shower. The textile becomes a window. Open the drapes. I desire to see and be seen. It is of no use. Only by plastering my cheek against the window will I be visible to a passerby. I can faintly see through the tinted window. From what I can discern, no one traverses the hallway. It is midnight.

I turn the television on. Through the thick walls, could my neighbors hear me scream? Through the hardwood doors, could anyone hear me bang? They are thick so no one can know what occurs within. If afraid, I would prefer to be outdoors. Not locked in a room or alone in a field. On a street corner. A block away, a store lit from within. Everyone is indoors by nightfall. The stores close at midday, reopen at three, and close again at five. Even they cannot work through the midday heat.

My mother appears in the bathroom doorway. We fall asleep alone but together.

We wake up alone but together. It is six in the morning. The light in the hall is still on but the sun is stronger. The warm rays flood through the crack between the drapes. I realize they are thick. The windows are tinted to keep the sun from making the room uninhabitably hot. The fluorescent bulb does nothing but cast light, unless I bring my hand to touch it. There is no one outside until the sun comes out. I hear men's voices and see their silhouettes as they walk past.

Pass the neighboring room on our way to breakfast. The Paraguayan girl in a maid's uniform is on all fours. "Her clothes are so clean," another guest admires. Her white cotton pants and shirt are starched stiff. My underwear is always clean because my mother taught me to wash them by hand. Yesterday's pair is hanging dry over the small window in the bathroom. Later when I pull it off the hanger it smells of meat. Behind the sleeping quarters is the grill where the steaks we have for lunch are cooked.

A tablecloth lines the buffet table. The clusters of beige flowers make it seem solid from afar and busy up close. A hardboiled egg with anise seeds for eyes, a crack for a mouth, and a sliver of lemon skin for a tongue atop a tray of scrambled eggs. The scene is reflected on a mirror that shows the contents of the trays below. Everything glistens: the tiled floor, the handles of the platters, the utensils.

We are seated under a painting of a storm. A barbed wire fence extending towards the horizon creates the perspective. It delimits nothing because the fields on either side are flooded. Thunder overhead is mirrored on the surface of the puddles turned ponds.

Leaves cover the tables, chairs, and floor of the outdoor seating area. I stroke the vein of a leaf. On the side that faces the ground it protrudes. On the one that meets the sun it indents. Both are red and speckled in black. But the side you must turn over to see is lighter and its secondary veins, yellower. If I lay it on my lap it covers my width. It is rough to the touch. Not the flesh of the leaf but the dry dirt caked to it. Inside someone cleans the potted magnolia tree with a damp cloth. One leaf at a time. They glisten with an almost plastic sheen.

The leaf fell from the *ombú* towering above me. The hotel was built to encircle it. I look up and see patches of sky between the leaves and branches. There is a metal rod dangling from a bough. One end is wrapped around another, making a hoop. It bobs up and down threatening to fall but never doing so. It is a warm day. But I do not feel calm. A parrot chirps noisily in the background and no one speaks except for us. It is not windy or raining. Nothing impels the leaves to fall. They all simply break free. There is something sickly about the branch.

I film the length of the main vein from the tip to the stem. The lens is so close that the image is blurred. The effect is akin to studying the leaf through a dirty vitrine. My forehead presses lightly and then harder against the glass. I still cannot see what I see.

Speakers on either side of the courtyard blast the booming voice of Padre Pedro: "The girls request veils for their first communion." I imagine a procession of young girls in white with stained yellow veils.

The Mennonites do not listen to the evangelical preacher's sermons. His voice indicates the proximate presence of a Paraguayan: the hotel employees, here, now. This is their country. Only they recognize it is mine too.

A man picks a branch out from the brick enclosed patch of soil where the tree sprouts. He wears a striped, yellow shirt and worn, gray dress pants with holes on the knees. Not a uniform. The rake and hose by his feet evidence his profession. He drags one end of the branch on the ground as he walks away and out of sight, into a shed.

A man in a cheap tuxedo, a waiter, I guess, steers a broom back. A raven mustache and a low hairline. It starts right above his eyebrows. Acne scars on his cheeks and deep wrinkles between his eyes. A face that transitioned straight from adolescence to old age. A transformation like that of the tight-pant-clad blond I mistook for a girlfriend in the dining room until his weathered and bearded face turned to meet mine, smiling oddly.

Keys dangle from the waiter's belt ring. He knows which doors they open. "The soil is dirty," he says. The gardener collects bunches of leaves in a bucket to be used as compost. He does not simulate attention or disobedience. Stands, half listening, his gaze straying to something on the roof and back down at the ground. They both disappear to the place behind the shack.

The waiter reappears in the meeting room. Assembles chairs along a long rectangular table outfitted with a white tablecloth. The pink tinged drapes are drawn closed over the four wall-length windows. The metal legs of the chairs cast shadows in opposite directions and intersect at a point. He sees us. Instructs we traverse the town from the first to the last monument. He traces the distance with his index finger on a map. A pen falls from his shirt pocket. Bends down with care. Pain is shooting from his knees. Picks it up. Resumes preparing the room.

The main avenue is wide. Two lanes in either direction. There are few people and fewer cars. There is the same tidy emptiness outside as in my room. Space between sidewalks is too broad. Where the Transchaco Highway merges with the avenue, a monument. A plaque at the foot. Inscribed in the stone, "Faith, Labor, and Concordance," and below it, "'What Jehovah has done for us fills us with joy' —Psalm 126:3."

Three cement pillars symbolize the core values of Fernheim residents on the colony's fiftieth anniversary. The cement poles are wider at the base. They grow tall and incline towards each other so the tips touch. The midday sun shines on the columns so the shadow of each reflects on the left face of the three-dimensional-triangles (tetrahedron). Two metal threads fencing in the memorial are linked to smaller replicas of the main poles. There are four of them. Each is inclined towards the center and casts a shadow to the left on the soil below. Cars encircle it as they enter and exit the colony. Trucks tilt as they turn. Their heavy loads threaten to knock it down.

A gated garden by the entrance into the town. The fence is adorned with two wrought iron trees. I see these twin pines on napkins, bumper stickers, and sliding doors all over the colony. It is the logo of the Fernheim cooperative. A girl rides her bicycle in through the open gate. A wisp of blond hair disappears. We follow her. Five *palo borrachos* encircle a tiled circle. In front of each, a blue trash can. Boughs sprout horizontally from the trunk. Twigs sprout vertically from the branches. They are bare of flowers and foliage. They once bore the fruit that lies rotting at my feet. It resembles an avocado. The thick green carcass encloses wads of cotton. Bury my nails in and pull out a clump. It smells of nothing except a hint of ammoniac. Leaves a sticky coating on the tips of my fingers.

I clean the rind out from under my nails with the tree's thorns. Most have been torn off or fallen. All that is left is the stump from which the needle used to protrude. Fingers rubbed the stumps smooth the way a statue's toenails are worn by those that stop to caress them. The skin under my nail beds is raw and sore. An allergic reaction to the substance in the cotton fruit. To tear my nails out would hurt. Pulling a sweater on overhead, the wool rubbing against the raw tissue when my arm traverses the sleeve, would hurt more. Eventually, the nail would grow back and occlude the tender spot.

A bush of pink roses by each *samohú*. They bloomed in winter and have started to disassemble. Their petals lie in a meaty pile over the sepal. When the wind blows, they fall. If they were not dying, I would assume they were fake. Something artificial about the blush color against the parched red soil and moistened black *palo borracho* trunk. The artifice is not reminiscent of the watering and pruning of the gardener but of the pesticide that coats it and fertilizer that runs from its roots to the tips of its petals. Still the flowers will only remain in bloom for a few days.

A branchless trunk wrapped in a thick metal chain. Opposite ends of the chain are nailed to two stumps. The nails keep the tree from bending with the northern wind. A copper plaque at the foot: "Monument to the *quebracho*. The resistance of its wood resembles the character and perseverance of the first Mennonite settlers."

The *quebracho* wood is exported from Fernheim. Trunks chained together to conform a single, massive tree are hauled on a truck bed from the colony, via the Transchaco, to Asunción.

We are not alone in the garden. There is a Mennonite girl atop a low bending branch of a magnolia tree. Reclining on her back with her arms weighing heavy in the air. Her friends take photographs with their cellphones from below. Her family would be embarrassed by the show. Not by her expression or clothes. Her smile feels stern. Her sweatshirt hides her chest.

A bush with dark purple flowers, the shape of horn bells, emerge from lettuce green stems. One is distinct. It does not enclose a wilting stigma, but another tightly closed lilac bulb. I pick it. It does not fit in my palm. Its petals refuse to detach from each other. But their tips, like antlers, sprout in diverging directions. Above the bush the leaves of a palm tree flail.

At the other end of the garden a woman. She sits on a bench carefully pruning the hedges. She extracts the yellow or brown leaves and sets them by her side. Soon there is a pile.

Through the gates that separate the park from the sidewalk I watch a woman approach slowly. She lugs three bags. The one in her hand is made of translucent plastic. Five sharp edged sticks protrude from it. They are about to fall out. The one over her shoulder is a messenger bag with a light peach colored flower pattern. It clashes with the neon green flowers on her blue skirt. She also wears a cap. The strap of the third bag is draped where the hat curves with her forehead. Its weight is carried on her curved back.

Behind her, at an even slower pace, a man on a bike. His legs take their time tracing a circle with the petal. Even when he is making progress forth his movement is delayed. He forces the maneuver left and then right. When the wheels reach the spot where the sidewalk curves, he steers it back. He never falls or drives into the back of the woman's knees. Behind them a multitude of bicycles. Small in the distance. Each making their way against the wind. Nothing to dissuade them. There is nowhere to stop and take shelter.

I stand on the opposite side of the gate. Peering through the metal rods. At the perpendicular sign by the entrance: "This is the Freedom Portal. The Founders of the Fernheim Colony arrived in 1930 fleeing the Soviet Union. A gateway like this one marked the border between the Soviet Union and Lithuania. This one is made in its likeness. It represents the liberty they attained by crossing its threshold."

Across from the park stands the museum. It is composed of three long buildings. Each from the early periods of the colony. Made of wood not brick. Narrow windows. Blinds of multiple slats. Though tightly encased in each other, they let the wind and dust in.

A woman is sweeping indoors in the first building. She straightens to attention at the entrance. The structure extends beyond the walls. A porch wraps around. The roof tilts to cover the tops of the windows. It is darker and the air feels thicker inside. Someone follows you in. They close the blinds and doors. A bellowing wind could do more than seep elements from the garden and road in. It could rip the slats off the blinds and the door from its hinges.

I push the window up and blinds out. A man in the distance is sawing a *quebracho* tree at its foot. Two men—one with a yellow hat and the other with a yellow shirt—and a woman stand by watching. The trunk eases its weight onto the missing chunk. It threatens to fall on the three spectators. The one with the saw waves them away. They drag their feet back two regular steps. He pushes the *quebracho*. The one with the yellow hat tilts his upper body left. It grazes his shoulder and upper arm. The woman's open hands rise to the height of her face. Outward facing palms. Not shielding her face. She appears to be pushing a phantom away. I hear the thump. All four disperse, unfazed. They abandon the fallen tree.

The museum I stand in narrates the history of Fernheim. A staircase on the face of the building, the only one with two stories, leads to the photograph gallery.

The walls are not wood paneled as they are in the other rooms but covered in wallpaper. The latter is stained beige with darker humidity patches. There are holes where the photographs were hung by nails when they were framed. Now they have been laminated and double-taped in place. The light casts a glaze that transforms them into mirrors from a certain angle.

On the back wall, images of the first Fernheim, Menno, and Neuland inhabitants, not as refugees, but settlers carrying out chores they no longer do by hand.

On the side wall, photographs of the cooperative buildings they built. They range in tone, dark to light; epoch, oldest to newest; and cost. Prefabricated duplexes—concrete slats are encased in steel structures—replace log cabins built by hand—layered logs are notched to lock where walls intersect. The solidity of the newest makes the first seem uninhabitable. They are all set in barren landscapes. No trees, grass, or bodies of water. The setting of the first looks like a desert. That of the last, a planned city.

On the opposite wall, the first meetings between the Mennonites and the indigenous people of the Paraguayan Gran Chaco.

The first illustrates a baptism. In the center eight men chest deep in the lake. They wear white shirts with stiff collars buttoned to the top. Two stand apart.

The darker man stands upright. He is not facing up, down, or straight ahead, but hesitant between the latter two. His closed eyes are beautiful. His nose is very straight. His thick hair is slicked back with sweat. His forehead and cheekbones glisten. His mouth is a tight straight line. You cannot see his hips. I imagine he will bend there when face and hair are submerged.

A boy on the shore stands directly above him. He holds something in his fist. He does not intend to throw it. The thing resting against his sweaty palm brings him comfort. A little stone or a cross emblazoned with his name.

The lighter man holds him up. Left hand on his chest and right on his back. He is furrowing his brow because the sun shines on his forehead. However, his facial hair nearly matches his skin, so I cannot tell. His eyes are so small they seem closed. There is a sturdiness to him. Though he stands straight his back is padded. His hair is like one large feather atop a bare skull. Where it ends, his little ears emerge. Behind him, not a shadow, a ripple. It marks his movement back and forth.

In the upper left corner, five boys look out onto the water from the shore. They must be about twelve years old. One hugs himself. The one at the front places his hands on his hips and shoots a foot forth making him more stable than the rest. The two in the back have their hands in their mouths. All tilt their heads in different directions.

All stare at those in the water. In the upper right, women and suit-clad men are piled into a carriage, each holds a parasol. The glaze of the gelatin image creates a stain atop their heads.

The shadows of both groups are cast on the murky, thus reflective surface of the river. The adults', a large formless stain. The boys', individual figures with long legs far apart enough to recognize them as limbs. A *palo borracho* looms behind them. Its denuded branches are entangled to make it seem full.

Three of the indigenous people that await their turn stare at the couple. I wonder if they are meant to look away. Two stare at the water. Their hair is not slicked back or to the side but cut short in the front, so there are tiny frames around their faces. It grows thick and long in the back

One looks forth. Nearly at the camera. He is the shortest of the six and stands in the middle. In the row his head makes the line indent. He is not younger but older. He is stumpy as in fatter. His chest is twice as wide as those of the children in the background. It is a matter of perspective as well as girth.

They cast reflections, not shadows, on the water. Smaller ones because it is only their torsos that protrude from the surface. Imagine their feet. Toes burrowing into the wet soil. One fidgets by wrapping his left leg around his right. Hand open and left arm softly swinging. The movement is barely perceptible. The sweet feeling of water between his fingers is invisible.

The second image shows two women with heavy loads on their backs and across their chests. The one in the forefront has the strap of one bag around her forehead and another around her neck. On her shoulders the legs of a goat. The animal peers over one shoulder. His white face, black ears, and front legs perked up. She wears a long sleeve dress. The black and white photograph makes it seem gray. There is a pattern on it. Perhaps tiny flowers or curled lines. Her legs and face are black.

In front of her, a taller goat. It is whiter than black. Beside it, a smaller dog. From the faintness of its coat I assume it is yellow. Another dog is walking into the bushes.

Behind them the second woman. She wears a checkered dress. As gray as the others. The load on her back is heavier. It strains her neck. Pushes her head forth and down. With one hand she burrows a cane into the soil. In the other she carries a long wooden stick diagonally. Like a gymnast on a high beam. It seems to keep her from tilting right or left.

Their feet are in motion. One foot planted far ahead of the other. They must be moving quickly. It is not their speed that blurs the image, but the upheaval of dust. You can see it rise around their ankles. The land behind them on which they walked is indented. As though a vehicle has trudged through creating a path. The background is full. The trees do not appear distinguishable. Except for one. Its leaves can be nearly picked out of the frame. The small mound from which the trunk sprouts glistens where the light touches the glossy material.

The goats are staring at the photographer. Neither the dogs nor the women look away from their destination or the dirt they trudge on. Perhaps it is the heftiness of the loads that makes them focus. Perhaps the photographer has been there a while. Perhaps this is the last photograph of a series and they have grown bored. They may just choose to ignore him or her.

The third image looks dated. All are black and white. The difference with this one is their clothing. Some are nearly nude. Others are covered. Their bodies are not discernible through the layers.

There are about twenty figures and all pose before the camera. The branch of a tree hovers over them. Two huts behind them. Straw roofs and a hay floor. Their amber color is a tone lighter than the black and white scheme.

There are four men in the bottom right corner with children on their laps. The face of the first is blurred as though he were shaking it from side to side in denial or disbelief. Atop the man's head a mane like the plumage of a crow. Caked in hardened mud. A lock sticks up as though the bones of a bird's wings keep it in place.

The one in the middle stares at the cameraman. His eyebrows are straight making his gaze stronger, colder, and present. Above his skull his hair spreads like wings. Drawing a diagonal from his forehead down nose and neck to chest. You can see they are aligned. His ribs jut out. Now he has his back to us. Now he faces us again. Arms cross but not in defiance. Hands lay open on the floor between his legs. He sits on the soles of his feet. His knees are spread apart.

The one beside him has his mouth agape. Hair caked like the body of a bird killed and stuffed with cotton. He wears a white shirt. Around his collar a necklace of feathers. Another face juts out over his chest. A man that lies on the ground before him. He wears a white hat with a ribbon around it. I cannot describe his face. Perhaps I do not want to. His features are so faint, hairless, and white. They match his placid expression. His fists press into the soil.

The last has his index on his lips. Smiles. Hair parted in the middle. Bunched at the sides. The shape of a drawn curtain. Eyes peering left. Neck and back arched. Hand behind his back as though to exaggerate the movement. He looks like a jester. The gesture hides what he feels.

Behind them peers the white handkerchief on a woman's head. There are no women in the photograph except for two. The second's face and torso are blurred. She moved or was pushed. This way her bare breasts do not show.

The three in the bottom left corner do not look at the camera or meet each other's gaze. One has longer hair and bangs. He looks to his left at the one staring at the floor. I cannot see his face, just his hair and clavicle. The lid of his left eye is covered in mud. His neck is barely visible. He submerges into himself with the same intention as he occupies his seat. He is an absent presence. The skin sags where the muscle in his left arm slacks.

Another looks straight ahead but his body is twisted at an angle. His arms are crossed around his knees. Not hugging himself, but burrowing his feet into the soil. His mouth, as though a crevice, is shaped downward on the sides. With his right eye he seems to be peering at the cameraman.

The face of the one at the front is distracting. His eyes have darted in such a way that your gaze searches for what he is looking at, outside the frame. What lies behind the cameraman? His hands are around his knee. He has a cloth on his lap. As though someone had laid it over him.

The last photograph depicts a railroad. Not a train car. Just the tracks. They show perspective. Between them there are patches of soil or grass. In the middle a stake pierces the ground. A sign, "One-way to Fernheim." In the distance there are trees. Black. Leaves and branches darkened by their proximity to each other. Further there is a pole from which cable lines stream. The clouds are still visible though faded. Parallel above the tracks, two lines left by airplanes in the sky.

We step out and onto the sidewalk. A poster of Ronaldo on a brick wall. His left leg thrust back. His face contorted by the effort or speed with which he must be moving but shuttered still by the photograph. You can draw a line from his foot to the ball knowing he will kick it. It will fly outside the frame. Below the poster, a yellow arrow. "*Entrada*" (Entrance) is the single word printed across the body. The door it is pointing to is closed.

Beside it, a vitrine. A cardboard wall behind the display. Ten shoes on individual shelves. The smallest is yellow with the Nike Swoosh in turquoise. Below them, a tiny disco ball revolving on a platform. It shines metallic lights on the shoes. In the opposite corner, a pair of dumbbells artfully leaning one atop the other. To the left of the shoes, a black sweatshirt on a hanger. Reflected on the glass before it: In the background, the bare tree in the median strip between two roads. In the foreground, a chain-link fence.

A large patch of yellow paint on the utility pole on the corner. The curves and dents of the wood grow more visible with the paint. It serves no purpose. Except to draw attention to the stop sign nailed above it. A white rhombus with a smaller yellow rhombus within.

Further up, another sign. A metal square with the posters adhered to it ripped off. I wonder how anyone could reach it without a ladder. It looms two meters above my head. I cannot see it unless I arch my neck. Then, my eyes meet the sun which forces me to squint. A single word on each of the three scraps: "Love," "Filadelfia," and "Search!" Each is typed in a different font and colored background. No way of knowing what the original posters said.

Behind the pole in smaller relational perspective, four yellow traffic lights. All face oncoming traffic. A single, red Volkswagen Golf slides to the stop sign until it turns green and continues.

Trees that waver in the growing wind. Sky billows with swollen, gray clouds. For a moment, things remain still. The clouds clear as though pulled by an invisible rope that accelerates time.

We continue down the main avenue. Buses emerge from the Mennonite secondary school. It stands opposite the Hotel Florida. It is three in the afternoon and the children have left. Four rectangular buildings encircle a large patch of grass. One is in disuse. The doors and blinds are closed. You cannot see what lies inside. It is an old house, as long and narrow as the new ones, but frailer. You can lift the roof with a strong wind. Wooden blinds over windows.

The effort to separate oneself from the outside was stronger, but less effective then. Even geckos could fit in the crack between the floor and the foot of the door. Imagine them climbing over the white walls. Their little paws aching in the damp air. One falls on its back onto the tiles. Its four little legs and smaller paws rustle in the air. He rocks his body to-and-fro. The left set touches the ground to impulse himself upright. He scrambles out of that dark uninhabitable space.

On the quad, there is nothing for the children to dangle off or climb on. There are two white arches. They are wide and made of wood. No net to catch the soccer ball when they roll it between them. I imagine the students sitting in groups eating lunch. There are lighter patches of grass where they sit. Their jeans rub against the blades.

You can peer into each classroom as you walk along the corridor that separates the buildings from the quad. They have large open windows. Distracted students can peer out but there is not much to distract them. I look out from that vantage point. Nothing is amiss, not even a plastic bag dragged across the quad by a gust of wind.

Shelves encircling the room are filled with students' notebooks and books. Pens and paper remain on their desks. Some have left their backpacks hanging from the backs of their seats. The furniture was specially made.

Between the legs of the chairs, a heavy block of wood. It prevents a boy from rocking back. He sits in the last row and rests his weight against the back wall. It falls away. The hind legs of the chair fold like the hoofs of a horse forced to bow by a *domador*. He falls on his back. The cold smack of the tiles against his spine.

A blue pencil case with the caricature of two seated girls leaning back to back. A crumpled sheet of pink paper on the floor. "Real weight," scribbled in English on the blackboard. On the other side of the room, a window. A similar scene to the one I stand in. But the trees are taller and closer together. Atop the objects in the room the reflection on the glass I am peering through. The bricks on the column reflect atop the black board. Above it a cardboard sign. I cannot read it. It is in German. I turn and see a bicycle.

Three men at a distance. They occupy the sidewalk. As they approach, I notice they are adolescents. They line up to let us through. Two are tall. One is short. The short one wears a large orange hoody and jeans that trail under his sneakers. No holes in his clothes, but they do not seem new. I am unsure of where they are heading from or to. They seem uncertain too. No one walks except for them and us.

The streets do not feel empty. An adolescent girl cycles by. Then, a middle-aged man in a truck drives past. They turn to adjacent streets lined with two-story buildings. Some have paved front yards and short metal fences, closed. Others, gardens with branches that poke through the holes in the fence to caress the passersby. No dogs, cats, or children playing outdoors.

Where the avenue ends, turn right towards a paved highway that leads to Neuland. Then, left to a monument that rises into the clear blue sky above a canopy of trees. We approach it slowly. A small figure stands by it. Four cement pillars. Slim at the foot and head. All slope towards a midpoint. The tips never touch. They are wide where they hold a cement circle in midair. The base is convex like a hill. A cross is rooted at the highest point. It is inclined to salute those that approach. Like a humble servant of God bending to the force of the sun.

The figure belongs to an old man. There is a thick bandage

wrapped around his white head of hair. An areola of blood seeps through the cotton. As we approach, he slips under the halo. He stands under the shadow it casts over him. He brings his body to touch that of the cross. Plastered against one another he peers up at the head and sky. Brings his hand to caress the tip, like a human face. The roar of an airplane invades the silence. It is small but so close.

Behind the monument a man-made lake. A fallen tree beside it. The force of the fall uprooted it. Like outstretched hands in a burning crowd, these crooked and dying roots search for dirt in the air. One branch bobs in and out of the moss-coated water. Ripples disappear and reappear. A girl sits on the furthest end of the bough. Her little legs push the lake floor away and move the bough up. Her weight forces it back down. She wears a large pink t-shirt, leggings, and flip flops. Black fishnet sleeves poke out from under the short sleeves. She cuts her mother's pantyhose at the thigh and ankle. They cover her from armpit to wrist. She sweats through the small holes where one thread of nylon threads over another.

A woman with hair aged white and sun stained yellow sits on the floor beside her granddaughter. The branch conceals her face when lowered and reveals it when raised. Her eyes are downcast. She stares at a stick insect crawling over a pile of twigs. Her hands remain on her lap. If her granddaughter fell in, she would have to place her hand on the ground to hoist herself up. The gesture would smother the mound. Bending over the lake she would outstretch a hand. The girl would grab hold. The grandmother would fall onto her back for her weight to gain enough momentum to pull the child out.

We leave them there. Neither noticed or acknowledged us.

Neuland

Magdalene Klassen, Frieda Müller's niece, walks through the sliding doors. Slender but prominent nose. Long, dark hair falling in folds down her back. Wide hips. Thin, when you stand beside her. Heavy, when she approaches you from afar. She smiles by accident. Peers down to hide. Tilts her head to the side. Looks out of the corner of her eye. Always greets you with an offhand comment. This time she says, "I am late. That is how it is." Suddenly and simultaneously I feel I am unkind to her and she is unfair to me.

I can stare at her because *you* speak on my behalf. You, mother.

I open the door to her battered, white Volkswagen Golf. A girl in the backseat. The face of someone that has been told she is pretty. Magdalene is driving Andrea to a boarding school by the Pilcomayo. She does not touch her. Pushes and pulls her with a sharp look or word.

Andrea slides close to me and takes my hand. Not afraid. Bold. There is a rashness to her movements that startles me. Her hand feels like my sister's when she was seven and I was twelve. I move and speak cautiously—or else, feel shame.

We turn onto the highway. It is five in the afternoon and getting dark. There are fields on either side. Cows brush the blades of tall yellow grass aside. A hunched spine that protrudes like a zebu's. The black and white pelt of a Holstein. No one fishes knee deep by the side of the road. Flash floods have not created ponds this month. The church, a square, brown brick structure with a tall yet austere, wooden cross on its roof, marks the entrance into

Neuland. Reach La Paz del Chaco and turn right into Frieda's paved entrance. The girl rushes in.

The air is stale and cool. Only the light in the study shines from within. There is a tasseled curtain over the door. A jaguar skin rug directly below it. The bulb gleams on the small cat's head, marbles for eyes. Andrea has set in motion the shadow the ropes cast on the spotted fur.

She lifts a leather desk pad revealing the contents below. Two photographs. One, a tall man's corpse held up by four men. The second, a closed casket. I know who lies within. Frieda's deceased husband, Walter. She lets it fall hiding what lies between the desk and leather sole. I was right to distrust her. Magdalene and her siblings are right to distrust me. Andrea and I were born in Paraguay, but we are foreigners in the Mennonite colonies.

Hear the girl run out to the car. Say nothing. Sit and swivel around to face the PC. A photograph of a boar by a man-made lake. The screensaver dissolves into a black background. Frieda took me there two years ago. Remember sitting on the wet soil and feeling no appetite. The boar and birds never came.

Everything is still. Watch the car back out through the cotton kitchen curtains until the bright, yellow lights dim. I step out to turn the porchlight off. Hear a bird's odd call. It sounds like shuffling feet but higher pitched.

Walk along the wraparound porch in the dark. With my right hand, trace the width of the concrete columns, and caress the bushes' leafage and blossoms. Turn and retrace my steps. With the same hand, check that the doors and the set of windows on each of the house's four external walls are closed. The windows are not made of glass but mosquito netting. They can be torn open with a knife. You can see through them from a distance. Up close the

39

threading creates a visibility barrier. I close the blinds over each. Not a frame with slabs encased. A solid block of wood. It keeps the soil out when the wind blows with force. They cannot be closed from within but opened while we sleep.

During the day I can turn to face the source. Usually find it vibrating. Lying in bed at night, I muffle the reception with one ear and measure the distance to the emission with the other. If you can imagine what causes an object to murmur, your eyes can remain closed. Measure the length, the low depth, when it occurs or recurs. Hear a click and hum, tell my mother it is the pump turning on and off. Water running, the tank filling. Rattle, the latch struggling to keep the blinds in place. We fall asleep to the sound of the droning wind.

Wake up to sunshine streaming in through the window. The wind must have turned the latch and forced the blinds. As my eyes adjust, I see the pattern on the *ao po'i*, openwork lace, drapes. Thin cotton threads pulled from the cloth to trace a mountain range. The shapes are darker where the fibers are missing. Three convex slopes of varying width and height intersect on different planes. Chubby clouds accumulate in the upper left corner. Pull them aside. See the tiled floor of the porch and the shadow cast by the pillar that holds the roof over my head. Lay back down with my feet against the headrest. The spaces where the air seeps through the mosquito netting gleam at me.

Mother's twin bed is adjacent to my own. A small landscape painting hangs on the wall above it. A hill curves into a lake. A dirt path lined with pine trees along the slope. A man by the side of the road finds shelter under a tree. He is small in comparison to the large shadow of the latter. The body of water is in the distance, if in perspective. If flattened into a single plane, it hovers like a cloud above the hill, man, and tree. This landscape substitutes what the roof and hedge of flowers occlude. I grow aware that I am in someone else's home.

I walk out. The wind hits me like a breaking wave. Not cold, but tepid, like bath water. The sun is not too bright yet because it is early. Weigh my feet down. Down the paved driveway. Light enough to see. The grass and bushes root the soil down. Still, the wind has bent the latter's branches away from where they naturally extend. On La Paz del Chaco Street there is no foliage or pavement, only dirt. It seeps into my mouth when I pull my hair from my lips and soaks the moisture from the corners of my eyes. Dirt tastes and smells like mud but dryer. It does not melt. You choke on it as you inhale or swallow, hard.

Beneath the sand the soil is as hard as pavement, even if cracked. The color depends on the proximity between the grains. Red if scattered. White if solid.

A caked dry and light patch beside the indent of a man's sneaker. A mark where the tip hit the ground. Four pebbles in disarray beside it. Another two further ahead. Where the cars accelerate— stop to let passengers out—or turn towards the main avenue, the density of the soil is altered. Perhaps more people walk down La Paz del Chaco than the surface of the soil evidences. The wind erodes their tracks nearly as soon as they make a dent.

Lawns separate the houses from the road. There are no sidewalks. Most have satellite dishes and all have water tanks on their roofs. What delimits the lawn from the road differs. A hedge of roses, an ornamental fence, a wall of trees. Most let the grass demarcate their property. No need to enclose themselves. The windows are tinted black or roofs swoop so low they cover the first. It is to keep the sun's rays out. Passersby cannot see the inhabitants. Yet the latter can choose to survey the first.

Walk to where La Paz del Chaco meets La Perdiz. A sidewalk

borders the highway. A man in a yellow vest sweeps loose soil off the curb. The wind lifts it into the air, against his calves, and back onto the clean surface. He stands in a cloud of sand. His motorbike still blows smoke. It is parked on a slope between opposing lanes.

Atop the small patch of thinning grass, a *palo borracho*. Its branches bend down to create a cocoon. It is not a shelter. See the accelerated sway of its shadow? The trunk as neck is lacerated. The canopy as head is severed. Whiplash. Before the leaves caress the crown of my head or a branch smacks me in the face, they sound . . . close. Recognizing their proximity may prevent me from enduring injury but renders noise ominous. When everything reaches a standstill, excitement ensues.

The fallen *samohú* fruit resembles a desert rose or a live one encased between parchment and glass. The texture of its green rind turned pale yellow is similar to an old woman's tanned skin. It does not droop off her face bones but creases into hard folds. The cotton pulp has been trampled flat by tires and soles but retains a few porous patches. The black seeds have escaped through those holes. They may be buried so deep the soil is moist and will sprout like the *palo borracho* they fell from. The fruit is encased in a patch as hard as stone. Six indented lines on the surface.

Animals burrow themselves in the soil to hide from a sandstorm the way you dive into a wave to prevent it from breaking on you.

Only what can weigh itself down is buried, stones and heavy branches. Twigs, feathers, and flowers are blown to a place where the wind hits a wall.

The southern wind breaks things: branches off trees, doors off their hinges, side-view mirrors off cars. Two shards of the latter lie on a patch of scrambled soil. The stone-like soil has been broken by force. Someone kicked the shards off the road to impede their sharp edges from puncturing a tire. One reflects the clear sky when the wind dies down. The other, my nose. If I grow close enough to exhale, it clouds and condensation covers my reflection. The wind is as warm as my breath, but it does not fog up the mirror. If I move, they turn silver and non-reflective. If I step on them, they shatter into smaller fragments. The reflection in each depends on its placement.

There are objects encased in the soil. A thick stick. Straight where it met the trunk. Bent where small twigs sprouted. I prise it out with my nails. The soil and the fibrous material of the wood burrow under them. Its indent marks the space it occupied in the road.

The same stick was used to carve a cross. It resembles initials drawn on still wet cement. I trace down, right, down, left, down, left, up, left, up, right, up, right, with my index. Not a vertical and a horizontal line that intersect. An outline.

An empty lot on the opposite side of the highway. Two large *quebracho* trees inside. A pair of sneakers at the foot of one. Black and gray with the laces undone. A plastic bag stuffed where the trunk parts into two main branches. Three vacant plastic chairs under its shadow. They are white except for the legs which are muddied brown. A radio on one. The extended antenna looms over the headrest. I could hear the muffled *cumbia* five blocks away. There is no one around except for the man sweeping the sidewalk. The return is imminent of those who fill the chairs, prop their feet against the trunks, sip *tereré*, and cut the acidity by biting into something fried.

I follow my own footsteps back to the house. They end at the driveway. I dwell in the garden. Behind the hedges the brushwood grows. Between the row of bushes and the pond is Walter's shed.

The hard-plastic roof is held up by four wooden poles but lacks enclosing walls. A single sculpture is left on the makeshift desk. A round base that curves out at the hips, in at the neck, and out at the rim. It resembles the foot of an ornamental table.

Plans for most of the objects he carved are drawn in pencil on the ceiling. Those erased to make room left a trace. The sun backlights the shapes. Measurements for the height and width of each piece are noted. The sizes vary. The shapes are so sloppily rendered that it only seems possible for them to acquire three dimensions if made of plasticine. The hand of the man that drew them was coarse, but it could force wood to take the exact form he desired.

Walter looked like his wife. Red and rough pale skin, especially around the lids, makes it hard to meet the gaze of their miniscule blue eyes. He was tall. Frieda, plump and short. He only ever wore a red jumpsuit. There is a photograph of him sitting with my mother and father by a fire. His face is inflamed by the flames and his arms are outstretched in gesture. They wear hats and smile wildly. There is a walkie-talkie on the floor. I can imagine it vibrate, crackle, and emit the voice of a fifth participant.

The fourth is the woman that took the photograph.

Remember Frieda hunched in the yard. Picking something off the grass. Turning to show me what she holds between index and thumb. The head of a snake. Its body coiling and unravelling in midair.

She reuses things the way someone litters. A plastic bag wrapped around a garden hose to keep it from sprouting water from a third hole. A red kettle at the foot of a tree serves as a pot. A single stem with two dying leaves. Hanging from an evergreen shrub, a tea bag. The bag nearly touches the ground but remains in midair. The torn leaves have dyed the white bag yellow.

Watch it turn on its axis until the light between the leaves distracts me.

There is something like someone indoors. Nearly see Frieda pulling a chair back from the dining room set and sitting with her legs open. The grid of the sudoku book before her is empty. She fills a unit with a number. Then, erases it with the opposite end of her pencil. Her small hands and mouth make her endearing in a disturbing way. Remind myself my mother and I are now the only occupants of her home.

Across from the table is a long shelf. On it stand Walter's sculptures. More sit on bedside and coffee tables, propped where two walls meet, or stashed in cupboards. They are not hollow. Equal their size in weight. The tiered trays seem made of clay. Platforms curve out, in at the broadest point, and up where they rejoin the central column. The pillars are miniatures of the faux marble one's on the porch. The resemblance is due both to the wood's growth rings and sturdiness. Yet some appear delicate. The small vases, though solid within, seem made of glass. They have a green tinge because unripe wood is more malleable. All smell of *palo santo*. A scent like smoke, if it was sweet.

Frieda collects other things. There are shells showcased in three floor-to-ceiling vitrines. Each is unique: one is rose colored with red stripes; another, yellow with nude patches, like an old man's discolored hand. All share the same sheen. She must polish them. What is coiled or clamped inside remains invisible. The largest has its own shelf on the wall. An open clam shell. The slick pink interior looks like a human palm. A tiny dried shrimp lies on the fleshiest yet hard part. Its tail curves to meet its head.

A cupboard connects living room and kitchen. Between the shelf with the good porcelain plates and the one with the assorted beer mugs, there is a third shelf. On it I found a little altar. A photograph of two hands nearly touching. Beside the image: a jar and an ornament. The first is filled with white pebbles and the space between them, with water. Something amphibious about the stones. The latter is a pink, clay flower propped atop a silver-plated sphere.

The sun has set. The room has grown dark. My mother and I do not acknowledge each other. Enduring the heat is easier when silent. I run my hand along the wall looking for a light switch. Feel something as frail as a communion wafer. Continue. Flick the switch. See a coral fan hung above the mantelpiece. The crack on the wall matches the shape of its main vein. An earring that once pierced Frieda's lobe is woven between two of the sea creature's veins like a fishhook.

The refrigerator and cupboard are empty. A handmade bag propped beside the trashcan. Two size ten jeans ripped at the inseams and sewn to each other. It is filled with sweet grapefruits. They are overripe. Mold adheres to the ones on the bottom. We tear the skins off, bite into the segments, and let the juice run down our elbows to the floor. I hug my mother. Regardless of how old we get or how much we ask from each other, everything is the same when we are isolated.

If our feet stick out over the armrests, we can lie head to toe on the two-seat couch. We watch a film on Frieda's tiny television. It is about a pregnant man. The buff actor is made to wear maternity clothes. We fall asleep once he realizes he is not growing a child but a tumor. I wake to a room lit by the fluorescent blue light of the screen.

A sound like someone spitting wakes me. It is coming from the living room window behind me. Then, the bedroom, bathroom, and study. It stalls in the kitchen. A woman is speaking a language I do not. The voice cracks when she repeats those five words.

Not talking to herself. Chanting. The way homeless people repeat what they said in the last subway car.

Light is starting to stream in through the windows. Each of Walter's sculptures it hits casts a short shadow. It must be dawn. Standing in the kitchen doorframe, I see a small silhouette on the porch through the cotton curtain. Mother opens the door slightly. A cold wind gusts in. The heat wave is over.

The stranger and Dolores speak in unison. The latter waits for a response. She receives none. The first's shoulders are quivering. Her hands run up and down her arms. I pull off the sweater I am wearing. Hand it to the woman. Watch her grow even smaller in the distance. She stops. Pulls the crochet blanket off her back. My pullover on. Her floor-length skirt, the streaked face of a tiger screen printed on it, flails in the breeze.

II.

Cayim ô Clim

A Bracelet

Everyone strays from the road. It extends from the paved avenue to a barren plot. A transmission tower protrudes from the horizon. A parallel line drawn by ten *quebracho* trees keeping an equal distance from each other. Four people traverse the crop. On either side the bush wood grows. Houses are fewer and temporary. Commuters turn left or right. Enter crouching through trampled paths.

The interwoven branches shield homes of cement or tarp from the northern wind. A breeze and particles of soil enter through the holes of the netted windows. Each house has a yard. Soil as hard as stone or brick pavement, little or no growth. Owners and neighbors meet there, outdoors.

A man in the shade and another in the sun. Both wear gray dress pants and colorful but faded soccer jerseys. They stare at the ground. The hems of their pants cover their ankles and fold over their shoes.

The one wearing dress shoes stomps his feet. Steps where the bricks separate the soil from the veranda. Alerts his granddaughter. He sees her playing in the bush.

The other wears crocs. The tip of his left foot dips into the sun. "I see your toes through the holes. They look like stones," says Felix. Yellow nails curl over the edge of the toes.

They watch a bottle wrapper flutter. One end is buried in the soil but the other floats. The girl watching them emerges. Runs past. Stops before the plastic sheath. Shields it from the wind until the free end floats to the ground. Stomps it down.

Juana is five years old or short for her age. Felix likes children that do not outgrow their parents. She keeps her back to him. Calls attention to herself but pays none to them.

She plops herself down. Shuffles her feet with increasing speed and force. The compressed soil breaks apart. She is digging a hole. The dirt that lifts off the ground covers her legs. Her heels chafe. Her mind is quiet. She imagines ropes around her soles tied loosely enough to tighten and rub when pulled.

A man towers over her. The one with brown dress shoes. Felix places his large hand on the crown of her head. She notices him when his fingers get stuck in her hair. It is matted and caked in mud. "Playing too rough," says her grandfather.

She cackles. Everyone laughs. The dust settles. Sore feet grow visibly immobile. Eroded colors change in tone. Her lime, floral print dress has grown beige.

The old men join their neighbors on lawn chairs. They offer them food that is dry—*chipá*, *mbeju*, and *sopa paraguaya*—or sticky—*guayaba*, ice cream, and soda when it drips and dries on your skin. Felix prefers *tereré*. It is bitter and does not taste like water.

Clothes that adhere to your skin, swift movements that make you out of breath and wet, or even a heavy bowl of something fried resting in a mound in your gut are unbearable in the sweltering heat. Felix only speaks, eats, and moves when he must and can.

Cumbia streams from a portable TV radio. A man addresses his mistress. Her undergarments show regardless of what she wears over them. They are alike. He looks unkempt no matter how much he spends on clothes.

The lyrics agitate the listeners. They turn to the girl for entertainment. She is tracing a circle around herself in the dirt with a stick. It leaves a faint white mark. Like dry skin scraped off. Presses the tip down in the middle of the ring. A full stop.

Juana does not crawl but hop to her grandfather. Her hands nearly reach the ground when her feet lift off. She crouches by his side. Hunched like an animal. Felix does not look at her. Sips from the *tereré* straw. Stares at what is in front of him.

She slips her hand into his pocket. It is not empty. Grasps a little ball of thread from the undone seam. Pulls until the pocket comes inside out. It breaks free.

She hides behind the trumpet tree. A low branch with five yellow flowers protrudes from the trunk. Juana strangles the stems of the blossoms in her meaty palms. Tears them off the branch. Rips off the gold petals one at a time. Braids the malleable stalks with the thread. Returns to the circle she traced. Places the plait atop the dot in the middle. Presses her wrist against it. Ties the spare ends. It means something to her.

Raising Angel

A cement square with two windows on opposing walls. One has horizontal bars on it and the other tinted glass. Sun streams in through the first rendering the latter translucent from dawn to midday.

Angel plays on the floor. Angela sits in the corner. The back of her chair rests where two walls meet. At the base is a pencil-drawn lawn or waves in a turbulent ocean. Both remain out of sight. Angel is Angela's grandson. They live alone.

He cuts people out of photographs in the newspaper. A woman, a man, and two children. Builds a home for them out of a box. The kids lie on the cardboard floor. Covers them with an article. The headline reads, "Hitmen admitted to sipping *tereré* with their victims before murdering them."

The cutouts act a familial scene. It is bedtime. Father comes in to say goodnight. Watches them pretend to sleep. Joins mother in the living room. They lean against a wall. Stare at a photograph of a mountain. It is a television.

The siblings tell each other stories. Until the listener falls asleep. The brother tells his sister about Gregorio. He exists. Lives opposite Angel's home. Works in the slaughterhouse in Neuland. Visits a Mennonite woman in Filadelfia.

He owns a motorcycle. Feels invisible and deaf when he drives. A cloud of dirt envelops him. The running motor drowns out the soft chatter of neighbors chatting on their lawns. No one knows how he can afford it.

He drives to Belinda's every day at midday. She fries enough *mbeju* to share with the visitor and feed her children when they return from school. They complain that it is hard and cold. She does not explain. They eat it anyway.

Angel tilts the carton on its side. Presses the open face against the wall. It is dark. The figures are asleep. He cannot see them but imagines their dreams. The boy crawls into a room. His sister and parents huddle in the corner. "What happened?" he asks. Falls into deep sleep.

It is what Angela does while she watches television that soothes her. Bathed in fluorescent blue light she tears the rind off an orange, divides it into sections, peels the hairy membrane off each carpel. She turns to the screen. Still holding the denuded orange.

Juice pools in her palm. It seeps through her fingers. Drips onto her lap. A stain will remain.

A child custody case. A mother pleads guilty to allowing her son to dress like a girl. "In his sister's absence he became her," she says aloud. The judge cannot hear her. She massages the pulp. Only the dry membrane is left. She dumps it into the bowl by her feet.

They sit outside at dusk. It is cooler. Angela has a deck chair. She arches her neck. Faces the sun. Droplets of sweat sprout from her hairline and drip down. Her sight is blotchy when she wakes. She sees a halo around the tree, the passing car, her grandson.

He seems himself when he plays alone. Stands in front of the window on the cement platform that encircles their house. Sees himself inserted in the reflection of the landscape. A *palo borracho* protrudes from the dirt lawn encircled by a thorn forest.

There are patches of grass in the soil. Gardens around ant

mounds. Each critter is indistinguishable. Together they trace a line to the entrance at the tip. It undulates. Some stray. Their failed uniformity renders them animate. Differentiable from a fallen twig.

He does not hear himself whisper, "It is hard to see things as they are." The interior is visible through the overlaid reflection of the exterior. A plastic chair below the railed window with an extension cord nailed to its frame.

The sight of the landscape through the railings is blocked by a tree that casts dancing shadows on the tiled floor where its branches intercept the sun. Angel's short slim legs twitch. He imitates the leaves swayed by the wind.

It blows from the south. Dismembers the soil. Creates a thick, brown haze. Bodies that obstruct its path claim it feels like dry hail. A hard substance in the air. Sand gathers to occupy space. The grains are close but separate. They do not dissolve into each other.

Angela's hunched figure appears in the corner of the frame. She is inside. Sees him daintily bend and straighten his legs. He sees her think, *he is effeminate and lonely*. The thrill of getting caught turns into shame. A scorching beverage swallowed hastily burns the roof of your mouth.

She stands before the stove. The water in the pot comes to a boil. A film covers the surface when it settles. She pours the oats in with the milk they secrete. It is a beverage and a meal. She likes to save time. It is all she has to spare.

The curtains are discolored and the wallpaper gapes in patches. When Angel was born they covered the barren landscape and cement wall with a lively pattern. "It is the sun. It is the humidity," she says of worn yet untouched possessions.

It feels cool and damp inside. Still a shelter from the unbearable heat. She sits back down on the chair in the corner from where she can see the boy disappear behind the wall. No one can see her. An old body finds stillness

Angel loiters outside Gregorio's house. It was painted white but turned brown. First in patches, where bricks were replaced but not painted. Then, paint chipped off those that remained. Dust gathered indiscriminately over the whole.

He encircles the building. Looking for something. Kicks the lower half of the wall. Rubble crumbles into grass. He finds it. Bringing his face as close to the stone as he did to the glass it does not become translucent but legible.

Miniscule words inscribed on brick. Short sentences follow one another. They are not poems but instructions. The author is anonymous. The intended reader, unknown. Words move the body of the latter and express the sentiment of the first. Disdain for the creatures who approach.

"Dive into the well. It is empty. Crawl into the tunnels dug to find water."

The diggers are as red as the soil and their fingers cannot unbend. They do not know what they want so they want what is in your fist.

A samohú *thorn? A packet of sugar? A string from the cuff of your shirt.*

Who wrote it matters. The owner of the house would not write on his wall. Where the pencil indented, the surface caved in like thin paper that tears. It is written with lead because ink does not adhere to a porous surface.

A nearly invisible act of vandalism. Only the child knows where to find the inscription. No one would suspect him. He follows the instructions. Walks to the well by the Cayim ô Clim monument. Notices a heart around two sets of initials on the blue pyramid.

It is dark within the cavity from which water is extracted. He hoists himself onto the rim. Sits with his feet dangling over the edge. Not the landscape of a valley below him but an unknown depth filled or empty.

He thinks of his grandmother sitting outdoors when the heat is bearable. The creatures in the depth of the well are not hiding but forced to remain where light and air do not reach. They want to be lifted out like infants. He is old enough to know he is not the intended reader.

He returns with the setting sun. The wind coats his clothing, hair, and flesh with the waves of lifted soil. Though he cannot see, he remains calm. It is what he refuses to see clearly that allows him to understand himself.

Nearly home, he thinks to himself. Overhears tense hushed voices. Then, a squeal.

Peers in through the mesh window. Gregorio is not home. The room is made large by the austere, widely-spaced furniture. A steel cot in the middle and a wooden chair in the corner. The roof is high. There could be a second floor or an insulating barrier of hay.

The day goes by. The boy remains alone and the woman indoors. They grow older.

Angel gets a job harvesting peanuts. He stares at the sun. Shakes lingering soil off the uprooted plants. Lays them on the ground. Lets the peanuts dry. Each brown capsule emanates a glow. He likes to think the halos are always there, and he can choose to see them or not.

Sombra Is a Horse

They call him Sombra because he materializes behind you at dusk. The horse substitutes your shadow. A distorted silhouette cast on the patch of soil shielded from the setting sun. An intangible extension, a limb, of a body that remains unnoticed until it disappears.

The outline of the animal protrudes in the dark like a body under a sheet. The Nujaché sisters watch him through their bedroom window. He sleeps standing under a *palo borracho* in their yard. They believe he is awake.

He is not loyal. Follows packs of strays into the matted forest during the day. They disappear. He cannot crawl into the bush. Only the top branches have thorns. He tramples them. Emerges with legs torn. The wet blood stains his white pelt.

The Nujaché sisters sit behind him, not fearing they will be kicked. Pick the dry mud and blood that coats his limbs. Stroke back the blond mane that covers his head and back. Comb his tail with their fingers. Grow bored braiding the long hair.

Usually, he is still. Nibbles on patches of grass like a sick dog. Swats flies with his tail or stiffens his legs so his muscles tremble. It reminds me that we eat horse meat. His mane is blonder and longer than the short hairs adhered to his flesh.

He is hard to look at when in the sun's glare. The warmest color is white. A flame that burns when you caress it with your eyes instead of your hands. He is dyed taupe by a coating of dust and indistinguishable when the north wind blows.

The children imitate him. Whinny and skip. They mount him. He shakes them off. When they throw stones at him, he becomes a stallion. Gallops out of sight. They leap onto the bumper of a passing car. Fall into the truck bed. Jump out when he slows down to turn onto Neuland's main avenue.

When they race back, they resemble horses, not a mocking imitation. A group of seven or eight. Faces distorted from the strain. They do not converse while they run but feel closer than when they share intimacies. Hearts pump with such force they cannot stop at the gate but climb over it and into the field. Some tumble onto the grass and cackle wheezily while catching their breath. Others just stop.

The children's parents trail behind them in a setting cloud of dirt. They are returning from work in Neuland. The Nujaché sisters watch Sombra follow their father through the gate and lawn but halt when he steps over the threshold. They play the game before it is too dark to remain outdoors.

The siblings search for something in the cloudless sky. "That speck is not the sun but an airplane," María Luisa says to María. The latter complies. She stares at the sun until the blood vessels dilate, and the white of her eyes grows red. The youngest turns to the eldest weeping. Asks, "Why do you make me cry?" María Luisa's face betrays her. She smiles so slightly.

María Luisa thinks she hates her sister because they share the same first name. They do not share the same father. María is blond and dark-skinned. Mennonite men stare at her. They do not wonder if she is their daughter. It is not hate but fear that she feels. María Luisa hurts her sister to make her aware that people do not mean what they say but mean something too cruel to say. What she forgets is that María has a temper and likes the suspense that precedes violence.

María recognizes cruelty and retaliates. She tears through María Luisa's eyelids with her filthy fingernails. María cries uncontrollably. The boys gather around them. María Luisa, though bleeding, picks her sister up. Cradles her with the force of someone older and whispers in her ear. What she says does not matter. María only and always complies to touch.

The Match

The dirt road is the field. The goals are four shoes. Two where tangent streets intersect. Each as far apart from its pair as the goalkeepers' feet. Imagine him with his arms raised and knees bent. His opponent kicks the ball between his open legs.

The players disappear before the game starts. Only the barefoot toddler remains on the field. He is meant to intercept traffic. There is none. A dog that looks like a wolf but slimmer and hairless stares at him. He lies languidly under a *quebracho* in his owner's yard.

Little Diego trusts strangers. Waits for someone to take him home. Lets himself fall softly on his bum. A short distance to the ground. Gathers dirt on either side of his legs. A ramp leading to his thighs, knees, and calves.

He lies on his back and waits for insects to crawl over him. His soles tickle. Neck stiffens and arches. Head hovers above the ground. He observes with minute attention.

An ant crawls through the space between his toes. Onto the top of his outstretched foot. Up his short, dimpled leg. Short distances traversed quickly by an invisibly small creature. He loses it. The ant crawls onto the hand the boy rests on his chest.

Diego places his palm on a rock. Bends his finger at the joint. Drapes its legs on the stone. The disoriented critter finds stillness. Then, sprints, elusive limbs, up and over the stone. Into the sand. It traces a narrow path the wind will erase. Reaches a mound. It is a city for those like him.

The dog continues to guard the child. They call him Lobo because he looks like one. He is not wild but domesticated. Recognizes where his neighbors live and when they trespass. Knows the boy does not belong on the road. Cannot call him by his name or take his hand in his own. Waits to witness what will happen.

He listens for someone crying, footsteps that are both hesitant and quick, the wheels of a car as they turn on an axis and go back the way they came. Wavelengths pass through him so that he can match the sound to the object that emits it. A surveillance video on in the background while everyone eats and speaks or smokes and looks through the window.

He is never indoors. Neither are the other dogs. When it rains torrentially, they huddle under the trees. The thorns burrow into their pelts and blood mixes with water. Their bodies adhere to each other emitting heat. Some copulate.

After a storm, puppies are born. At first, they resemble chicks. To move would mean to fall from the nest over a precipice. Then, they follow the mother around suckling on her teats. Eventually they stray in separate directions.

Sometimes the dog bores the child. He mounts him. It lays down and rolls on its back. He dismounts. Now the distance between them does not collapse. One warns with a glare.

Still on his bum he spits into his palm and mixes it with sand. Dribbles the paste into cone shapes that stand on their own. Decides most are pines and some are tents. A village in a forest. Where it is cold and the people are tall. Sand is only sand, but these people exist elsewhere in the flesh.

The boy is staring past the dog at a woman bathing. Jacinta is dressed. Bends at the waste. Plunges mane and forehead into a bucket of water. Lathers with soap. Soaks it. The blood drains to her head. Wrings it like a thick cloth. Combs her hair back to front. A heavy curtain over her face. Sweeps it back. One gracefully aggressive movement. Undoes the knots. Her mane glistens free.

Bees fly around her head and come to stand on her roots. She smells sweeter than coconut or vanilla. Suckle on the strands that sprout from the holes in her head. Do not prick the scalp that separates them from the skull. She remains still and waits for her hair to dry.

The frigid well water creates goosebumps along her biceps and forearms. The sun soothes. Skin grows smooth and warm like the now tepid and placid water in the bucket. Her eyes are closed. She is like a horse. Falls nearly asleep standing.

The tips reach the backs of her knees. She smiles. Realizes she can tickle herself. Traversing the tall grass, she tries to distinguish who touches her. The tip of each blade reaches a distinct height. When the wind blows, she feels enveloped in a wave. Knee deep.

There is something bubbling below the surface of her routine. An ambition. To go beyond the confines of the Nivaklé settlement and even the archipelago of colonies. To be unlike her mother and father, not greater than them. She already is.

When asked why she remains unmarried she answers that no one has asked. It is a half-truth. The unwed men of Cayim ô Clim do not ask. They know she will marry a foreigner. It does not occur to her that she has enough money to board the bus to Asunción. She will not find this man working in the corner store. He will find her.

The other women admire and pity her. They do not comb the

caked and matted nests atop their heads. Children pick the strands apart with little fingers. Lice find crevices under their nails. Live there until they die or are prised out with the sharp edge of a bottle cap.

Odd how cutting a strand does not hurt but pulling where it connects to your scalp does. Is this a taste of childbirth? A body extracted from your own. Cut the umbilical cord or deliver the placenta, feel nothing.

Diego does not recognize Jacinta. She is his neighbor. The house behind her is her own. The one beside it is his. She rescues him daily. He is too young to be always alone.

Hers is a small and simple brick structure. The drapes behind the windows are floral. The colors are toned down by the strength of the sun. Not red and moss-green but a beige-pink and gray. The light is always lit from within. Hushed voices and the rustle of small bare feet or long skirts sweeping the floor.

She lives there with her mother and father. They are even-tempered and quiet. She mends their things. Where their clothes tear. At the knees and elbows. She suspects they crawl and purr like cats when she is working at the store. They do not. It is where their legs and arms bend when they sit in their armchairs.

Every thing outdoors has become useless. Glass shards mark where a bottle was smashed. Lost keys never fit into the locks they were meant for. Plastered tin cans hold no liquid content. Even the air within has been compressed out. The corner of a rug is frayed. Outside the unit it belongs in it does not adorn but litter.

They taught their daughter to exist apart from them. If she leaves them, they will care for each other. They are not cautious. The towel is on the floor. The tiles are splattered with grease and honey. The backs of their leather shoes are bent so they become slippers. It is not lethargy.

It is the best they can do. Use what they own until it disintegrates. Have a daughter to watch her go. The problem is that materials grow thin, crack, or fray. Do not disappear. Jacinta grows tired and restless at the same time. She stays.

The man strokes the woman's hand and she smiles without looking up from her lap. Unlike the uncompostable materials that contain what they eat and drink or the home they inhabit, their bodies will decompose underground.

Jacinta watches them before retreating to her room each night. Never thinks about love. They are together. She is alone. Thinks about codependence and convenience instead.

The man she will marry will be red-faced with blue eyes that glare like the sand when smacked by the midday sun. The lightest colors are the warmest. A flame transitions to orange, yellow, and white as the temperature increases.

He will not stroke her hand but hold it. Lead her into a parked car. In the sealed interior, she will see he is smaller than her. His long thin fingers will stroke her side. She will not impede him because she will not feel it. He will be unlike anyone she knows. The problems will start after knowing him.

There are voices coming from behind their home. The windows look onto the main road, not the backyard. The elderly couple remains indoors.

It is the boys, arguing and dividing into teams. They have gathered behind the windowless wall. Huddled in a circle except for the one that stands apart. He is always in the way.

They call him El Chico. It means both boy and small. His father started it: "I can't go into the kid's room." "The kid used up the last of your glue." "The kid has a splinter in his toe." They named his siblings Jesús, María, and María de los Ángeles.

He makes instruments out of popsicle sticks and twigs. The corners of his mouth are perpetually dyed orange and his molars are full of holes. He does not taste the orange flavoring, the ice turns his tongue numb, but sucks until the heat within subsides and he has the missing cog.

A miniature pot and ladle, a stove they will not burn on, and a hunched figure that resembles his mother. A scene like this one for everyone he knows. He breaks the wood into slivers. Weaves the unmalleable materials together to create the bases. Sharpens the end of the stake.

The small, yet life-like, tools and characters litter the floor of the room shared with his siblings. Before his father comes home, he shoves them under María's bed. Except the crucifix. Jesús uses it to clean between his teeth. He knows not to swallow it.

El Chico now carries it in his pocket. When unsure, he feels it. If alone, he takes it out and imagines that man is his older brother. While he thinks, the boys grow silent. Divide into teams. Forget he is there.

On one side they are fast but scrawny. On the other, strong but fat. Those that are not fast or strong know it. All except, the one that was sick in class, Elviro. He emanates a smell. Pretends not to know why he is chosen last.

They run in mass towards the empty street. Out from behind Jacinta's home. One kicks the ball. It lands with such force that it makes a dent in the soil and remains still. The first to reach it is the one that kicked it.

Diego remains in the middle of the street turned football field. Staring at the woman's head tilted towards the glaring sun. Still waiting for her hair to dry while her skin grows moist with sweat. It is the light that is making her thoughts buoyant.

Feet sweep past with screams or cackles. The ball flies over his head. They are light because they react quickly and when they run both their feet come off the ground.

Jacinta opens her eyes. They adjust to the light. Cries for the boys to stop. Everything is still. Her voice resounds like an echo. The toddler crawls to where the dirt road curves up into a lawn with patches of grass.

She takes his hand. Leads him into her home and places him in a newspaper lined fruit crate under the table while she peels potatoes on the surface. His lids twitch like one who feigns sleep. All Diego can control is whether he sleeps or eats.

The boy tilts the crate and crawls out. A bag of flour on a low shelf. Punctures the thick paper with his sharp nail. It pours onto the brown tiles. He cups his hands under the stream of white powder. Brings them over his head. Separates where his fingers touch. It pours over his head. He licks his index. It is sour. His pout turns into an audible open cry.

The boys scream when they play. They do not hear Diego stomping his legs against the tiles or Jacinta whispering, "Nothing happened, Diego. Nothing will happen." Picking him up and cradling his little body, which fits in the nook of her arm. It soothes him. He falls asleep with his head against her chest. Afraid of setting him down she stays, standing, for what feels like hours.

They only see the white ball turned yellow and mended with scotch tape. While it rolls in either direction it is their feet that they see. Imagine it at an angle moving towards the sphere, colliding on a given spot, setting it in motion, redirecting. Other feet try to intersect. Shadows extend where legs end.

One running in a straight line towards the arches, faster than the rest, calls out "Elviro!" All turn to see him in the way. The runner dodges around him and scores a goal.

The trick is to recognize your own feet. After that it is only a matter of being fast. They cannot outrun the dogs. Ball escapes the court. Past a liver-ticked one. Teeth pierce the thick fabric. It deflates. Plastic covered leather carcass lies lifeless across his large pink tongue. They turn back, stray in different directions, and disappear into their homes.

His mother has come to carry him through the still swinging mosquito-netted door of their home. Jacinta sweeps the white powder off the tiles and runs a wet cloth between them. There are clumps of saliva moistened flour in her hair. She does not see or touch them but her head feels heavier.

This is motherhood, she thinks. Knows she wants a child of her own. When the place where her stomach reaches her pubic hair swells, she will never be alone again. Thoughts of the red-faced man and the cold interior of his car dissipate. She wants any man, one that will leave her and her child alone, together. What she has not had he will have.

It looks like rain. She walks into the man-made lake. Feels the ground under her feet, and the water covering and revealing her body according to depth. It is unlike the sea. There are potholes below water. Land caves in where gathered stones were displaced.

The surface does not break onto the shore in the shape of a wave. It remains a flat plane but tilts like a ship pouring what it cannot contain onto the encircling platform that is the land, spreading thin into the distance in every direction.

Her surroundings grow visible for an instant. The encircling thorn bush. The highway leading to Filadelfia. A bundle and a pair of sandals by the rim of the lake. Lightning is followed by thunder.

All is dark and wet. She has to remind herself to feel the rain. Even when it pours each drop lands and drips, softly. Lightning strikes. It takes a shape as indiscernible as a misremembered dream.

A head of slicked back hair emerges from the tilting surface of the water. A man that smiles with thick lips offers the woman an outstretched hand. He opens his fist. A smooth black pebble rests on his palm.

Like a bottom feeder he caresses the floor of the lake, searching for stones. He opened his eyes underwater. In the dark, through the murky liquid and gravel sweeping past his eyes, he saw the girl's feet planted underwater.

His thick voice cracks when he says, "Jacinta." She is not frightened but sure. He is someone she knows. She takes the stone. It feels heavy in her palm. Her body feels light in the water.

She floats onto her back. He imitates her. They cannot see the stars or moon. As dawn breaks and the rain ceases, they return to their feet. Walking alongside him the dirt does not adhere to her wet skin. Water runs over the surface carrying with it the loose sand that would envelop them, were the soil dry. It rarely rains.

Not Sinking but Floating

Water accumulated where the highway, on a platform of soil, curves into a lower road. Now it is a pond. Four floating bodies. They are not hot, thirsty, or filthy. Just want to feel nimble and powerless. Their torsos surface. Limbs sink and curve into odd shapes.

They shed their shirts and shoes as they neared the water. Red and white jerseys, and black plastic sandals scattered far apart on the dirt road. A car drives past. Cloud of upturned soil. Tire marks on the clothing. One of a pair of sandals plastered into the earth like a fossil.

A boy climbs up and out of the brown water, Benjamin. Bum dips in as hands and feet burrow into soil. It is like someone is pulling at him. Not from his shirt but waist. He swats behind him. There is no one there. Not even the water. Only air. His wet back glistens.

There is a fallen tree. A *palo borracho*. Its big womb rests on the ground. Roots upturned by the hole where they were once burrowed. The narrow part of the trunk and thinner branches do not touch the soil. They reach for the sky. The leaves are turning brown and falling off.

He grabs hold of the end of a thick, barren branch. Steps where it meets the trunk. Uses his weight to push up and down. Pries it free. The limb lies by the dismembered body.

Picks off the few green leaves still left on the twigs. Weaves them into his wet hair. Cups water in his hands and splatters it atop his hot head. Mane and foliage cake together and bake in the sun until the still wet strands turn hard. Not a crown of thorns, a helmet.

Cuts off a side of the branch with his rusted knife. Hollows out the interior. Concave like a cylinder sliced in half with closed ends that curve up. As long as his arm but wider. He rests it on the water. It is a canoe.

Before it floats too far he places it back on solid ground. Fills the interior with blades of grass. By the fallen tree lies a nest. The eggs within are cracked and the chicks seep through the shells. Deposits them one by one on the bed of foliage.

Rests the toy canoe with the unborn chicks on the placid pond. "If they cannot fly, they might as well float," says Benjamin. It drifts past his friends' heads or feet. They remain still so as not to overturn the vessel.

He stands at the edge. Crouching so his torso floats above the pond. Each time he exhales rings appear on, and dissolve into, the liquid surface. Water is generous. It reminds him he exists even when he is still. He wishes the air was thicker and less translucent. Not to impede sight and movement but to render it visible.

Water slowly seeps into the ship and open shells. They sink, becoming invisible in the muddy liquid. He assumes they lie heavy on the pond floor.

Silence. For a moment, no one's feet touch the ground. One is mid dive, forehead nearing the surface. The others are on their backs, soles graze the air.

He shatters the calm. Waves flow over the rim of the body of water and overturns the four floating bodies. A flame is sparked between the ribs that cover their lungs. The place where things that must be regurgitated go.

A laugh makes a strange, painful noise and a kind of hysterical excitement begins, making the swimmers squirm like eels through muddy water. They are not intentionally imitating the fish they resemble. Thought halts and is substituted by action.

They grab the boy that tries to escape by the ankles. Once they have torn him from standing to lying on the pond floor the game is over. He emerges laughing and the excitement subsides as all return to restful floating.

Warm bodies turn tepid and white rays, red. The sun is gone. They remain. They do not see each other but touch themselves. Wrinkled fingers stroke sun burnt stomachs and foreheads. Their necks are wrinkled too.

The black water mirrors the dark sky. Reflects the stars and moon that faintly trickle light. Benjamin feels oppressed between opposite planes. Reminds himself they are convex. The earth's core is as far below as the sky above.

Tunnels can be dug. An underground city built. It would be cool there. A sky, like the one above, painted on the soil ceiling. There is water below. Water towers pump it into pipes that, like tunnels, traverse the impenetrable interior of compact soil or concrete walls.

He dives into the deep, dark pond, headfirst. Penetrating the membrane that marks where water substitutes air. The others imitate him.

Sunken bodies outstretch and spread arms. Bend and outstretch legs. Propel themselves forth. Reach the rim. Press palms against solid ground. Arms tremble. Feet land. Toes curve in. Torso and legs bend and straighten. Four figures stand straight. Still for a moment. In motion, again.

They dress and run home in unison. Diverge one at a time as they reach a familiar concrete or impermeable cloth structure. Hungry boys. They devour what is left for them. Swallowing or inhaling water does not substitute the intake of food.

Benjamin's grandmother waits for him on the lawn. She sees best in the dark. No one can see her. Tells her grandson a fox ate his ration of meat. Benjamin does not mind going to bed hungry if he can give the old woman some pleasure. Amalia likes to tell stories.

"I set the plate on the ground. He emerged from the thorn bush. Quietly yet quickly approached the dish. Nibbled on it to check for bones. Bit into it like an animal. Swallowed it in viscerally large chunks. Then, disappeared."

They search for moving figures in the dark. Then, retreat indoors. It is like a tent with cloth walls that do not cave in. Four steel rods onto which the canvas is tied taut create straight barriers from outdoors.

They lie down. Next to each other. He turns to her. She is the last and first thing he sees every day. The skin hangs off her cheekbones and falls in folds along her neck. He imagines dust gathers there. She is so still, asleep.

He dips the corner of his shirtsleeve in his saliva filled mouth. With the tips of his fingers, softly lifts the widest fold of her neck and brushes the moist cloth along it. She exhales with force as though perturbed by something in her sleep.

He knows she dreams of being a jaguar. Light brown pelt with black irregular spots. The costume conceals her from prying eyes while she hunts small cats. They resemble her kin but move less swiftly and have blunt teeth. Grasps one by the loose skin of its nape. Its weight hangs where her teeth dig into its pelt but do not tear. She drops it in her lair.

Caresses it with the soft pillow of her palm. It nuzzles into her paw. Mistakes it for the face of an animal its own size. She brushes its slobbered pelt off its forehead. Its tiny lifeless eyes gaze up. An expression of fearful dependence.

He does not want to imagine her biting into that slim neck. The cut pierces the carotid vein. It tries to shriek but the inaudible open mouth resembles a yawn. It feels weak, cold . . . drifts to sleep. Benjamin halts. Rewinds the movie in his mind.

She pauses when her teeth burrow into the fur. They pinch the flesh. Her head tilts back. She plants her paws and prowls through the tunnel in the thorn bush, back to the denuded lawn. Drops the screeching cat and retraces her steps.

Her brow furrows and the corners of her mouth twitch. She has feline features, like his own. Eyes that curve up, a wide nose, protruding cheekbones, a thick long mouth, and teeth hidden within.

She was beautiful when she was young. She told him so. No dated photographs to prove what she looked like or know her age. She is who she is now. He believes her. It is true now if it was not then.

He hears a rustle. Twigs swept aside. Then, stomped on. Soft thump. Two sets of paws against the solid bare ground. A sound like water. An animal brushes against a wall of the tent. Seeking contact

Benjamin brings his hand to the canvas. Feels the shape and height of the dog's body. Its thumping heart encased in an unpadded rib cage. It paces back and forth. Not like an animal encircling its prey but a human being searching for an entrance.

The frail tent separates him from the external noises audible indoors. The words used to phrase this comforting thought turn until they lose all meaning and he is asleep.

He does not dream. Thoughts occupy him the way immobile critters, edifices, and figures inhabit the world outside these frail walls.

Darkness encompasses everything inside and out. The dog has fallen asleep curled by the side of the tent where he can feel Benjamin's warm body through the canvas. Not even he is keeping watch.

Before daybreak Amalia wakes. The boy's face is so close to her own that his features merge together and she cannot distinguish nose from mouth. He emits the calm of someone never forced to do what he does not want. She feels this before recognizing him.

He refuses to participate or obey by fleeing. Neither confrontation nor contagion proceed. He just chooses to be alone. The rest of the children abide by the teacher's or leader's rules. He drifts to a place where he can watch them play or learn but is not in the way.

There is nothing but pain in her face. Each morning her sight is blurred and back hurts. If she moves the pain contracts and stays in a single place. She remains as still as when asleep so it comes in waves, spreads from where it originates and dissipates.

She looks at Benjamin's extended body. On his back with outstretched arms and legs. He falls asleep later to occupy her place when she wakes. He uses space wisely, does not sacrifice comfort or displace the other.

His other siblings, mother, and father, occupy the two rooms in the brick house by the tent. He is the eldest. Amalia grew used to his way of being. When the others were born, she tried to hide her disappointment. They were different. They clung to her.

When he was a toddler he never stayed by her side. Would play games that appeared dangerous but always proved to be about self-care.

Once, he dug a large hole. Climbed in. Dragged the dug-up dirt back in. Only his head remained above ground. Stared at his occluded body as though forgetting he had buried himself. Made a small oval dent in the soil with his still free hand. His bellybutton filled with tiny particles.

Laid his head down on the bent arm using his hand like a pillow. He stopped perspiring. His body felt cool underground. His face was under the shade of a tree but still felt the heat. It was useless. Drops of sweat poured from his forehead.

She never feared for him. When he took risks, he did so to meet his needs. By three he already knew he wanted shelter from the heat.

He opens his eyes. Amalia sits on the ground by the opening in the tent door. She is studying the shapes on her dirty soles. Through the crack, he discerns it is still dark out. A cool morning breeze seeps in. Hunger and cold wake him. Not a wholly unpleasant feeling. He feels alert and detached.

Crawls towards and past the hunched figure. Things look the same in the morning. People sitting outdoors do not seem suspect but entertained by others. Animals congregate but still hang around humans. Trees and homes are indifferent to the people within and below.

Only the road looks different. Less narrow than in the dark. What the night enveloped on either side, peering eyes and towering structure, seemed to encroach the small but discernible passerby. Now everything is open and nothing seems to occupy enough space.

Amalia makes her way from her bum onto all fours. First to stand on her knees and then bend so her hands touch the ground. Through and out the opening in the tent. Crouching beside him her soles replace her toes as her base.

She pulls the bag of bread out from behind one of the flaps and places it between them. He feels the rolls and takes the one that is turning stale. Sucks on the hard crust, bites, and swallows the moistened chunk. He produces no waste. Eats what will go bad first.

When his stomach swells and his head feels light he rises to standing and sprints so far down the road he is out of sight.

She tears the soft crumb from her still malleable roll and kneads it with her warm hand. Molds a male figure with a head, neck, torso, arms, legs, and feet. Props him up by the door to dry and turn hard, unless stolen by a famished dog.

A plastic bag dangles from the branch of a nearby *palo borracho*. "Panadería El Paraíso" is printed across it.

Disintegrates the piece of bread left. Rubs it between index and thumb. Crumbs mark a path back to her tent. Not birds, but dogs lick them off the dry soil and blades of yellowing grass.

She crouches and steps through the flaps. Lays herself down. Curves her back into a half circle. Curls her legs in. Her pain and thoughts cease. She sleeps from midday to sunset.

For those five hours, she traverses the bush beyond the town. Purrs as she scratches her back against the prickly trunk of a tree. Devours the meaty flesh of a fallen mango but leaves the pit. Lies under a thorn bush to watch the children play but keeps a distance. Just the scent can make her ravenous.

She wakes when the sun is setting. Nothing edible left. The scent of grilled meat seeps in with the breeze. The light of a fire glows through the canvas wall. She watches her family through the open flaps.

The flames turn their cheeks red. Their eyes flicker as the father says something true. Attention diverges from the speaker to their meal. Their heads pull from the slab of meat between their teeth. Tear a chunk from the whole. Chew in silence, swallow, and speak.

It is dark when she steps outs. Feels neither cold nor warm, hunger or thirst. Needs nothing. Her mind is lucid. She sees things that are not there. Make them move towards her. Speak and touch her. Retreat. The one that makes her feel least alone approaches.

Holding Hands

The girl on the wheel-less bicycle fast approaches. It cannot roll so Claudia raises the handlebar to her shoulders and drags the rear steel poles. They leave a deep indent in the hard soil. She makes a noise like a horn that alerts Juliana and Sarita of her presence.

There are four of them, sisters. Two that hide behind their neighbors' house. Staring out at Jacinta, the woman by the ditch. Both have their hands in their mouths. Nervously biting nails and, when there are none left, fleshy fingers.

Their clothes are torn and dirty but colorful. Juliana wears a black sweater with pink sleeves and yellow sweatpants. Sarita, a maroon sweater with hearts embroidered along the cuffs and jeans with bird patches on the knees.

Their hands are always touching. Holding a wall in place or a toy standing. They fear things will fall apart or topple over. They are accustomed to feeling what they see. The sand riddled wind is always palpable. Entwined fingers recognize the touch of the one beside them.

Their hair is straight and combed but in disarray. Juliana's got entangled in a branch and the bun on the back of her head pulled right leaving clumps loose on the left. She has a flower behind her ear like the yellow one in Jacinta's hair. It is pink and the petals are broader.

The bloom looks like it is made of cloth until she places it on her tongue. It tastes like dust and disinfectant, but the petals disintegrate between her teeth like thin slices of mango.

Juliana stares at hands and feet because she cannot decipher the expression on Claudia's face. Her thick eyebrows rest on her lashes and the black oval pupils seem to peer out as much as they sink in. They do not express fear or even distrust but a kind of curiosity that knows no bounds.

Persecuting, being persecuted, or pretending to be someone else is more than just pretend. They flee from her when playing catch, she hides while someone seeks, animates a doll by moving her and changing the tone of her voice.

She only acts in order to draw closer to what she is staring at. Once she watched a man, like a shadow, crawl into the thorn bush. She dropped to her hands and knees to follow him in. Her mother spotted the little figure under the white prickly branches and dragged her out by her feet.

Their feet are never still. Even when standing the ankles bend and the tops touch the ground. Sarita can never keep her sandals on. When she runs, she steps out of them. It is a trick that does not please mother. She would let her go barefoot were there not shattered glass along the road and the rims of the wall-enclosed homes they climb into.

Juliana, Sarita, and Claudia are waiting for their mother and eldest sister, Gabriela. They watch them walk through the dust along the main road to the settlement. The eldest is more beautiful than they will ever be and there is a pride in that.

Holding Her Hand

Their bond is based on filling the silence of running errands. Sometimes the conversations that fill it are straining and they return exhausted.

Gabriela's skin is luminescent because it stretches tightly over her cheekbones and is covered in sweat. Even the dirt that sticks to her cheeks and forehead gleams like the scales on a fish. Roberta's is a murky river.

They both wear Lycra. It soaks in the salty water and makes their bodies perspire. It also reveals the shape of the flesh it covers. Folds under the mother's arms and breasts. Curves along the daughter's hips and chest. Both women are more visible than when they are nude.

They traverse avenues and side streets. Always at the same pace. What changes is the speed of passing bicycles and cars. One stares at the ground and the other, at the sky. They do not see the storefronts, homes, or thorn bushes to either side.

It is only when they cross the street that they look towards incoming traffic. Nothing encroaches the sight of the end of the road where sky meets the land. The electric cables weaving from pole to pole lead the eyes there.

What they see is the horizon. It encloses colony and settlement. Hushed, complicit voices. Gabriela carries her bags like they are weightless. She swings her arms back and forth. The opposite side of her palm caresses the wind. The way it does the mane of their dog.

They carry rice, cheap cuts of meat wrapped in cellophane, beer, and sickly acid sweets. They travel to the Siemens supermarket, not the Cooperative. Mother stands behind daughter. A barrier between the young woman and the men lining up behind them.

Proximity is indiscernible when there is intimacy. Hands graze. Fingers intertwine. Choice invisibly substitutes chance. Sometimes cuddling surprises more than groping. As a child, when she felt self-conscious around company, Gabriela dug her nails into her mother's bicep. Now Roberta rests her weight on Gabriela's forearm.

Sometimes Roberta glares at her daughter. She misses her youth and all the things she never had. Height, a sense of humor, eyes that stare at the sky instead of the ground, flesh that does not sag, feet that do not drag, and legs that sprint on demand.

They talk about small things at first. Roberta points, not at the floor, but at her foot. The bone overgrowth where toe meets sole. She tells her daughter you do not stop growing when your height ceases to increase. They remember the grandmother who sprouted a new set of molars at one hundred and five.

They notice the ground. The intersection between streets they step on the dirt road. Gabriela says she feels her feet bounce. She wonders if it is hollow below. As they step onto the sidewalk Roberta skims the tip of her enlarged toe against the pavement. Does not stop or notice.

The aftertaste of water boiled in a burnt pot. How the kettle refused to whistle that morning. The family waited around the table until it was time for school or work. The contents of the kettle evaporated and its sole burnt. Without something to keep or make hot, it self-destructed.

Gabriela and Roberta guarded the water until it came to a boil and made their morning *mate*.

They improve the lives of the family members in small ways. Set a box of matches atop the toilet all six share. The scent of burnt metal exceeded that of *yerba* so a match can occlude the smell of excrement. It is like covering a grass stain with a coffee stain.

They laugh at Alberto's private shame when he realizes the box is meant for him.

Each morning they collect water and hand wash the whites. It is the midday sun and not the soap that removes stains. From the window, they watch the clothes flail in the wind. Sometimes, despite their efforts, things get worse. The dirt adheres to the shirt and socks turning them brown.

It filters in through the open door. A doorstopper made of cardboard folded to make a rectangle. Horizontal sloping side creviced between the wood and the tiled floor. The hinge on one side is loose and when encased in the frame it must be lifted to revolve open. If the girls are playing inside and the elders leave their home, they are locked out.

They spot the tall woman and her stout counterpart slowly approaching. Claudia drops the handles and lets the bike fall on its side. The other two run out from behind the wall. Excitement burgeons from the possibility of frightening mother and sister.

They tread softly even when they run but there is no one else around and the children, though closer to the ground, are discernable at a distance. Roberta feels joy and dread at the same time. She is too old. Wants the young to care for her. Their excitement turns to anguish when felt by her, still their joy exists independently.

All five make their way home. The girls run ahead. Raise a short cloud of dirt behind them. It only dirties the hem of their pants.

On tiptoes the three peer through the windows. A *mate* gourd and a half-eaten pink glazed cookie atop the green apples and pear screen printed plastic tablecloth. Stained yellow sheets crumpled atop two unmade queen beds and a twin.

The door is jammed. Roberta tries lifting and pushing. It is the lock she has forgotten to open. The girls grow impatient. They tear open the sour sweets and sit on the steps resting their small backs on their mother's and sister's heels.

Roberta has always been slow. Slow to understand, in school. Slow to return an insult with a quip, at work. *If they slowed down,* she used to think, *I would understand, respond, do as asked.*

Instead, she became kind. Responsible, never neglectful, especially with her children. She raised them to move at her pace. Speak in hushed tones, you cannot speak quickly when you whisper. Never run, you will not get hurt. Ask permission, even to eat or use the bathroom, they will call you polite.

Only the eldest obeyed. She is one person alone and another with Roberta, no one else ever accompanies them. Her mother weighs her body, tongue, and mind down.

Gabriela takes the key from the hand that offers. She turns it, grasps the handle, lifts it off the frame, and pushes in with her hip. It smells like the ashes left after a fire, but everything remains as they left it.

The girls rush into their room. They lie on their stomachs with the sandals dangling from their toes and then falling to the ground. No one can hear what they say because they whisper.

The scent of grilling meat and boiling starch interrupts their conversation. They are back around the table as they were this morning. "The rice tastes like burnt toast," says Sarita and they hear a match flick on and off in the full toilet bowl. All laugh.

Juliana, Sarita, and Claudia rely on their mother, and Roberta relies on her eldest daughter. They never feel alone. Gabriela fears leaving Roberta. The latter, being by herself. She thinks she will give into herself. Remain motionless, unable to eat, speak, or move.

Not everything is up to them. Especially not the wind they see lift the soil off the ground and envelop those commuters still on their way home. Only the sway of the trees retains comfort. They waver but rarely fall. Deep rooted like Gabriela to her mother.

A Rock Like a Drop of Water

The tree in the ditch is taller than the two-story house next door. Dug so far underground even if you peer over the rim you cannot see where the trunk divides into diverging roots. Ricardo and Lourdes can pull the leaves off the lower hanging branches. The horse can caress those on its crown.

A dove flies overhead. Amalia sweats a handful of crumbs in her fist. She scatters them, leaving a trail. It is not the birds but the dogs that will lick them off the dry soil or few blades of yellowing grass.

Every day after lunch she sits on the ledge. Dangles her feet over the hole. Imagines it is a pool instead.

A woman floats by her. Belly up. A spaghetti float interlaced behind her back and under her armpits. They do not touch but the water is redistributed between the two bodies. It rises to one's knees from her calves and carries the other over a wave that regains stillness before it breaks.

Copper hair floats around her head. Ends extend in opposite direction from the root. Her cheeks are chubby and rosy from the sun. A tiny button nose and long lashes that curve nearly over her lids. For a middle age woman to be so cute is nearly obscene.

Her name is Lena. She has three adolescent sons. She ignores them when they misbehave. They are playing football in the field nearby. Still wet and in their swim trunks. The dry dirt adheres to their hairy legs like a crusty scab. It is not the games but how they play them that makes their hearts race.

The eldest sits in a chair watching nearby. They tie his legs to the chair's. Two heave his body and the piece of furniture atop their shoulders. The trick is to run and pass the ball to one another without dropping the boy or losing the ball to an opponent that encircled them.

They grow dizzy and faint from carrying the weight. On the count of three drop to their knees. The eldest reaches the ground standing. He resembles a gymnast when she dismounts the balance beam.

Once untied he runs after them. All four jump into the pool. They splash the woman sitting on the rim and capsize their mother. The latter dives to the base of the pool, emerges with her hair slicked back, and climbs out. She smiles but instructs them to follow her indoors.

This is not all in Amalia's imagination, but memory. When she worked at a hotel, after growing bored of her chores, she would sit by the pool, cupping water in her palms and splashing it on the crown of her head and the back of her neck. She did not like to swim. She liked to watch.

No one told her off though the beds were rarely made and the rim of the toilet bowls were yellow with scum. She did not mind the filth and assumed they would not either. When the owner's children and wife went indoors, she would pick useful things from the lawn.

Little yellow flowers among weeds. Uprooted them. Placed the still dirty stems behind her ear. Found and kept a fifty Guaraní coin. It glistened in her dark pocket. Felt the outline of a face. A dignitary carved into the flat steel circle.

Once she found a ribbon. It had been white but the rain and

dirt turned it the pale yellow of old worn silk. Tied it around her ankle. Each time she took a step forth she peered down. A quiet dignity in the adornment of the hairy end of her limb.

She always dressed well. Still does. A worn liberty dress on top of a plaid skirt. A thick wool belt with woven patterns around her waist. Brown leather shoes two sizes too big and worn without socks. Her daughter bought her sandals so her feet would not sweat and turn callous. She never wears them.

Yellows and blues and oranges that make her brown skin gleam. Even her white hair turns gold with the sun. After eating she picks at her teeth. It is vanity. A piece of rotting meat cannot be lodged between such a white and straight set.

Sitting on the ground removing dry, dead flesh from her hardened soles she watches birds as they pluck twigs from between blades of grass for their nests, the chicks extract food from their mothers' mouths, prise apart their feathers when they are wet, fluffing them up as they flap.

When it is time for a snack, she likes to drink Fanta straight from the bottle and eat the crackers made with animal fat that come in a translucent package. She picks them out one by one. The fat glistens in the sun. Then, the remains shine on the tips of her fingers. She licks it off because it still tastes like salt.

Her mind races after she has eaten. It is the heat. Blood pressure drops and *su cerebro se siente mecido en el cráneo* (her brain feels cradled in the skull). Light becomes something to watch. She places her palm on the top of her head. It is boiling. She could crack and fry an egg on it. Still she likes how her mind works when she has sunstroke and is underfed.

Everything has a halo around it. Her sight allows her to choose not to see what she dislikes. The house, children, and man of the house blur. The ants grow clear. They work hard to make a home for themselves though someone will trample it soon and they will have to start again.

She can feel the texture of things. Her rough but taut skin, sharp nails, long strands of hair that curl at the root but then grow straight. She likes everything about herself. Even the scars on her knees from kneeling on the stone encrusted soil while staring at things no one seems to see. Sometimes she leans against a rock and does not notice until she sees the trail of blood.

Her attention span is both shorter and longer than most. During conversation she grows distracted by the things happening around the speaker. That is why she cannot stand crowds. So many people speaking at once. She has to listen to them all. They are crying out to be heard. It feels terribly sad. No one can hear and understand them all at once.

It was worst when her children were young. There are five of them. It always felt like she was in a crowd. She loved them and that was why it hurt. There was no way of giving each the same amount of attention and so she would feel bad for one while resenting the others. The chosen one would alternate.

They never understood this and instead felt that one was seen as being the most interesting until he or she grew to bore her like the rest. There was an element of truth in this too. At a certain point they stopped thinking of themselves and started worrying about her.

With time she has become more and more solitary. Drifts towards the hotel where she no longer works. Encircles the fenced-in courtyard watching for nothing in particular. Returns home to eat and then sits by the old sunken tree in the lawn. She rarely speaks and they stop expecting her to listen. Ironically, their home has grown louder and happier.

Her grandchildren are dropped off and stay for weeks on end. They follow her. Climb atop her lap and fall asleep. Play with her hair and their food. She never tells them what not to do. It is tranquility, not love, that they feel in her embrace.

Like a child, she keeps secrets. Smiles at a stranger while her grown children speak among themselves. Then, pretends not to see him when he smiles back. Grabs hold of someone's hand even if it is the least-liked wife of one of her sons. It is the stillness with which she reacts to their stupefaction that sets the tone.

Still there are the thoughts she thinks to herself when alone. Mostly they regard things she would like to make. A door stopper so it does not screech and remains always open. The children run in and out making her head ache. She wants them there. Does not want to monitor their movements.

Birds Plead When They Sing

Piedad places her hand on the sack tethered to the tree's thickest branch. The bottom fits like a tiny bum in her palm. Pushes the stubborn weight. Releases her grip. It sweeps through the air seeping flour through its seams.

She does not own a yo-yo. With the index in the thread hole release the encasing. It coils back. She does not own a dreidel. Turn the tip by grazing index against thumb. It turns on its axis and falls on its side.

Her toys react to touch. A snail on a leaf. Slimy, pale body contorts to slide forward. Tentacles with eyes on the tips stretch in opposite directions. She pats the little head with her digit. It retreats into its home. Below it on the sand lie ten empty tortoise shells. A cemetery and its keeper.

Its weight forces the leaf to turn on its side. It slides onto the sandy soil. Surrounded by tortoise shells. She collects them by the river. Keeps them under the bush by the tree instead of under her bed. They stink of still adhered flesh. The snail creeps into a dark carcass.

Piedad blows on the now loose leaf. The force of the air must hit it at a certain angle, so it turns and wrings the stem. It grows limp and bends where it remains attached to the bush. She crouches to its height. Peers between adjacent branches. Exhaling in its direction. Her hamstrings ache.

She sets her playthings in motion. They react in slightly different ways each time.

She amplifies the facial expression of her playmates. The slightest curling of the lips and brow expresses endearment or annoyance. She cannot tell the eyes from the mouth. Decides they have stopped playing the game and resorted to mocking her.

Playing alone means she can repeat herself and stare. Discover the objects and critters that surround her. They gain autonomy with the caress of a human digit. She taps them again and again until they cease surprising her.

Behind her the collapsed tent where Mariano lived. She lifts it from the center where the three cloth triangles meet. Reaches for six branches gathered behind her for firewood. Places one under each seam. The tips of five fit where the broadest stick splits.

The structure holds up the tarp. She imagines he remains within and that it is raining outside. His home is made of impermeable tarp, but the water still seeps in, between the seams. He sits directly below the leak with a bucket in his lap.

When the rain ceases, he soaks his feet in it. His skin is always burnt red and covered in a layer of dirt. Dead layers of flesh do not flake off but remain buried under other substances. He does not act, scratch. The desire does not subside.

He never feels truly still. It is his skin, not an insect atop it, that crawls. He lives with the itch, the water that seeps from the roof, and the people that enter his home like it is their own. There is nothing ominous about it. Instead it is a familiar discomfort he is as fond of as the boredom of old age

He watches the dirt detach from under his nails. Feels his toes unclench. Before slipping his sandals back on, he rests his soles on the surface of the water. His large callous feet look like boats. His ankles, like sails.

Mariano collects the things that float away. What can be mended or used to mend. He likes needles the best. Finding one means he sees everything. The tarp of his tent is stronger than the rest. Square patches of cloth are affixed to the laminated plastic.

The tall grass is a barrier. Bristles stop objects in flux and store them. He understands how an object moves. Weight indicates the height it will achieve. Shape, what it will entangle itself in. Desirability, who will run after it, human or animal.

They call him El Peine, when they do not call him El Loco, because he combs through the grass. He also catches bits of his neighbors' conversations. He listens most closely when someone has lost something, a job, a girlfriend, a parent.

It is how things can belong to someone and then only to themselves that interests him. They do not last long on their own. Of all the things he has found and lost few continued to subsist waiting for him to find them again.

He is attached to what he keeps. At night he turns and sees the pile of newspapers by his head and an alarm clock not ticking on top of them. Finds use in what has lost its intended purpose. Uses food wrappings as ornaments and broken toys as interlocutors for his nightly conversations.

Before he passes away, he decides to build a fence. Mariano picks up his axe, takes an impulse back, buries the steel edge into the hard wood. The tree does not fall back but forth. He bends back so slightly. It nearly grazes his face. Only a stump with a sloping surface is left.

All the trunk's arms are chopped off and the body is divided into pieces. The broader ones for firewood. He piles them in the center of the yard where the bonfire will blaze at night. The slimmer ones become stakes.

He jabs each stick into the soil at an equal distance to the adjacent two. The bodies of men, women, and animals fit between them. It is not meant to keep them out but delimit the area where he lost the stone.

The land around his house belongs to him. On hands and knees using a feather he sifts through the loose grains. The rock resembled a drop of water. The same sheen and size but when he pressed it between his fingers it kept its shape.

All it took for him to grow obsessed with finding it was to forget it for an instant. He had it in his palm, as weightless as a thorn, was holding it up to the light. Above it he saw the crown of the *palo borracho*. Atop a thick but high branch, his daughter, Emilia.

He ran to her. Dropped it. Stood below her. Ready to catch her if she fell. He was helpless. She had to choose to climb down. Burying hands and feet lower down the branch and trunk she let gravity weigh but not force her.

He smacked her with the back of his hand. Then, realized the palm was empty. This did not anger but sadden him. The girl cried. He did not hear her. She needed an explanation. He provided none. His obsession grew until he was alone but surrounded by objects others lost.

Something underground trembles and the tent collapses again. The sticks protrude like bones under the gray tarp. Others use sheets instead of impermeable tarp. The water soaks through them but the floral patterns remain.

Cloth gives the wind shape. Concave when it blows against it. Convex where it seeps in and out again. The material gapes over the underlying structure. Between the folds there are shadows.

Through the fabric the silhouettes of the inhabitants shifting within are visible.

Piedad collects the sticks. Grows to standing. The sack is directly above the crown of her head. She does not collide with but graze it. Aware of the objects that surround her even when she cannot see them.

Takes hold of the sack with both hands. First feels the plastic bag, strand over strand woven into a tight net. Then the yellow corn flour within, when she presses her finger in, the grains accommodate to a new shape. She remembers the *mbeju* her mother made.

A flat, flaxen cake sliced in three. Dry between index and thumb. A dusty film covers the surface. It tastes of flour, pork fat, and cheese. The latter is sour and ingested in clumps because the mixture is not whipped thin.

The round sits lightly on a metal plate. Mother, brother, daughter take a slice. A blue goldfish appears on the bottom of the platter. Its little fins protrude from its swollen body. They seem to flutter keeping it in place.

No fish in the murky ponds, well, or puddles that gather where the soil indents when it rains. The large silver scaled *carimbatá* her grandmother remembers is meant to be eaten not admired through a thick glass bowl.

Piedad forces herself to eat. The familiar discovery of an animal under a heaping meal is her reward. She feels hunger but prefers to feel light on her feet. Her limbs move at a quickened pace when she refuses to concede to bodily needs.

Carmen forgets what she wants and does what she must. Calls Piedad. She leaves the kitten in a cardboard box under her bed. Helps flip the *mbeju*. Sweaty hands covered in thin, silver hairs.

Both stare with contempt at the kidney shaped mound of rice and the curved sausage. White beads of starch glisten because they are coated in oil. Matte fat exuded through the lining on the pork is cold and has turned white.

She holds an open bread bun in her left hand. It resembles a gaping open mouth. She places the sausage between its soft white lips. A red tongue that exhales hot steam and a scent that renders her hungry.

Carmen's gaze is on her hand. It rests atop the fork. Its prongs on the rim of the plate. She does not prick the food. A fly crawls along her index, onto the utensil, and into the heap of white grains. They are only slightly larger than its body.

Her mouth is wide and her eyes are far apart. The bridge of her nose indents where a line can be traced between them. The part in her hair is growing broader. As she ages the follicle from which a strand was uprooted does not sprout anew.

The man beside her is her brother. Carlos has his mother's features but a rounder face and hair combed back while it is wet. His mane sprouts from his eyebrows. It does not make him look dumb but worried.

He pricks the sausage. Bringing the brazen red shape to his lips he bites off the end. Squeezes the bun between his four fingers and palm. Turns it towards Piedad and makes it speak. The words he utters do not matter.

She retaliates by propping the sausage atop the rice. When the side of her fork presses into the meat the grains fall onto the table. A heap forms below the sides of the plate. She brushes them off and onto the floor which the dog licks.

They do not speak but mean what their gestures imply. They feel the absence of someone but also a sense of calm. It is like walking home alone. Boredom and dread make the time it takes to get from here to there longer.

Piedad sees the face of the missing man. Not at the table but in the memory of a photograph. He has a film of thin hair on his upper lip. It is meant to be a mustache but is mistaken for the residue of a frothy drink.

The flour sack remains still after she releases her grip. She sees three figures across the lawn. A man and two women walk towards the bus stop. Turquoise skirts graze their ankles. Heels tread on his gray slacks.

The man is pigeon toed. Thigh and foot bones curve in. Knees protrude under gray cotton. Toenails stretch the leather of his black loafers. A pigeon's feet and red eyes are as frightening as the visible distortion of a man's bones under his flesh.

His pace and posture are deceiving. He walks with intent. Stares at the floor. Appears pensive and determined. He forces his body to respond to thought. The sole must not land on the roof of the opposite foot. Peers up when his toes curve over the curb.

The three figures are still. They are waiting. The man tries to tap his foot to express impatience. The heel rests on the floor. His hard-tipped shoe does not strike the beat of plastic against pavement but atop skin, animal or human.

One woman is bow legged. Her thighs never graze. They stem

from her wide hips which she grips firmly with large hands. A defiant stance. The distance between her firmly planted feet betrays the gap her long skirt conceals.

The other's knees knock together. Heels do not touch. Places weight on one foot. Leans left and forth at an angle. Plants her other foot down, regains balance and repeats. Her body does not bend when it moves. A beauty in her stiffness.

Their shadows differentiate them. A triangle, an oval, and an hourglass. Light only seeps between the man's legs. Neither relatives nor neighbors, just passengers. They visit the Mennonite hospital every other day at midday.

The rumble of incoming traffic is mute. There is none. Drivers fear their tires will burst. Pavement burns light like white sand. Cars rest under tin roofs. Adults rest in rooms rendered dark by thick drawn curtains.

Only the child with calloused feet remains outdoors. The water underground renders the dark soil cool. Piedad's brother and friends have crawled into the thorn forest. She does not see them but knows they surround her.

Imagines she is flying low above the forest. Below the frail white nest of branches small figures advance. Brightly colored clothing differentiates them from animals. Six bodies. The one in the coral shirt leads. The rest stray but move in his general direction.

Her brother's shirt was red but grew stained pink by the sun. It catches on a thorn and rips a little. The forest pulls and tugs but does not tear their flesh. It is their un-calloused knees that strain against the grains and rocks in the soil.

Carlos is slimmer and shorter than the other boys but always knows where he is going. The games he invents are hard to follow. Others imitate him but remain unsure of the rules. Only he knows they are searching for the *tajamar* where the *taguas* sip water and roll in the mud.

He loves the hard, brown bristles on their hulking bodies. How they glisten when the mud dries, cracks, and falls away. How softly they step with their tiny paws. Almost ridiculous that those short, feeble legs can carry such a large head.

The males are all snout and tusks. A line around the neck marks where the ribcage starts. Hair along the spine always stands on end. Little legs bend at the knees. Eyes are rooted so deep in their sockets they seem fake. As small in proportion to its build as those on a bear.

Small eyes do not render the animal or man harmless or dumb. They just express less emotion. Face to face with an animal of this size the boy feared its pulsing weight. If it made an impulse forth it would trample and maul him. They remained still. The latter retreated the way he came.

On their hands and knees the boys snort loudly. A long-drawn inhale that exudes a resonant vibration. It feels like the land under their paws trembles but it is just their bodies. Short choked inhales follow. To Carlos the first means follow me and the second, retrace your steps home. He forgets to tell the boys.

Breeze carries speech across the lawn. The pitch of a man's voice sinks, he falls silent, a woman's cracks and interjects. Piedad feels complicit because the natural cadence of their voices is hushed.

The man says he hears nothing. The woman says she does. They look to where the road meets the highway. The rumble of an engine and a cloud of dust. A bus slow approaches.

Upturned destination sign on the roof, "San. . . ." It trails off illegibly. Lopsided Mercedes Benz emblem on the black bumper. Uneven road surface makes the body incline right. Gold tassels rim the front window and obscure the driver's face.

Words and yellow crescent shapes hand-painted on the elongated tin body. "*Pasajero*" (Passenger), under the numerous sliding windows. "*Conductor*" (Driver), below the windshield. On the back, "*Nunca estás solo. Mirá para atrás. Mirá al costado.*" (You are never alone. Look behind you. Look beside you.)

White letters rimmed in black. All capitals except the first are in a larger type. Where the shapes curve in or out, the black line curls. Dirt covers the body, windows, and tires of the bus rendering them indistinguishable from the soil below.

A hole by the driver's seat replaces the sliding door through which passengers enter. A current of air sweeps in and out the back window, ajar. It rustles the driver's hair. Everything gets small.

Piedad hears the porky driver pant and the gold cross smack the glass.

He emits a low droning tune with a restrained but fluid exhale. The words seep through the open door. They grow intelligible when they reach the still girl's ears. First, she feels the sadness. Then, understands why.

Something sprouts from the inner right corner of her eye. It slides down and around the nasal fold. Reaches the right tip of her lip. She gasps for air. It slips into her open mouth. The tear dissolves on Piedad's tongue. It is salty, not sweet.

Pleading he sings, "*No llores, llorona. Estás hecha de azucar y te vas a derretir.*" The crying woman's flesh is made of sugar. Tears melt the compacted white particles leaving trenches where they slid down her face.

A woman's voice streams from the bus radio, "*Cuando lloro siento que me lamés la cara.*" She asks him to lick her face featureless.

The driver takes his hand off the wheel. Wipes his forehead dry. Between the fatty creases drops of sweat and a film of dust gather. If the salty beads drip into his eyes they burn and render him blind.

It is the heat, the monotony of the slim road, and the encroaching thorn forest that makes him fall away from the body in the seat. Even the music bellowing from the speakers reminds him of being elsewhere. A single word separates dreams from daydreams.

Passengers waiting on the sidewalk are as miniscule as flies. It is the twitching of their eager bodies that forces him to see them. He cannot discern their eyes from the blurred features of their faces but feels their burning gazes.

Behind the settling cloud of dirt, the hulking white carcass of a bus appears. The driver pants and the vehicle trembles. Thinks how cruel he is for riding this old horse, tin and bones, from Yalve Sanga to Cayim ô Clim.

He can speak but waves instead. Passengers pick their parcels off the ground. Bags like the one that held flour are crammed full of *ñandutí* cotton squares, *caraguatá* fiber purses, and *tagua* fat elixirs. Carry what they will sell and packed for an overnight stay.

One carries a cross. It is in the palm of her closed hand. The chain entangled around her wrist. Another, a photograph. Folded in four it fits in his shirt pocket. Creases along a young girl's cheekbones and forehead to chin. The last, a brush, an old shirt, and a pair of shorts.

The driver outstretches his padded palm to the knee knocked woman and the other pushes her bony bum from behind. Three steps mean she must bend to lift each foot and place uneven weight on the still straight leg. Where her knees meet, they chafe.

Their hands do not touch her where it hurts. They acknowledge that she feels pain. Once seated, legs remain outstretched, feet fall to the sides, but toes point towards her face. Feel a release in the back of her leg like the crack of a chicken's neck.

Three profiles in the side windows. The bus reaches the corner and tilting turns left, then right, and left onto the highway. Faces inch just above the rim of the rear-view mirror. They comfort the driver because they are there, not because they are familiar.

Piedad remains, alone. Imagines she is on the bus after it disappears. Wrists lean atop the black, red, and white plastic bag. Wringing long fingered hands. Her bones ache before a storm.

Extracts an old cotton square from her parcel and a needle painted blue from her wallet. With the latter she picks threads from the first. Grasps it between index and thumb to pull. It leaves a line through which horizontal strands intersect.

Threads so thin and woven so tight they are invisible. Single vertical strands stem from the dense center. Filaments intertwining over and below them are missing. Single horizontal threads intersect. Rings that grow further apart as they stray from center.

Fingers that swell at the joints and bend at the tip. Hand that scratches, presses, bends, and tugs to make a piece of cloth emit the resounding sound of thunder or a heavy object plunging into a deep, dark body of water.

The flour sack continues to swing. It is the wind instead of her small palms. Pink, yellow, and gray disembodied shirts flutter on the rod between the house and the adjacent *palo borracho* tree. The encroaching *quebracho* trees shudder but the solid trunk of the first remains motionless.

She breaks a thorn off its bloated gut. A brown husk exterior like dry flesh. Where it meets the trunk the raw orange tone of new flesh. Indented trenches on the base. Irregular ovals like the shapes on a map.

It is weightless. She forgets what she holds. Drops it. Sharp end down. Buried in the white earth. It resembles a man's sole. Head and body underground. One foot un-buried. He fell from the sky. Not like the pick-up line: "Did it hurt when you fell from the sky, Angel?" But like a shot bird.

They hunt doves in the Chaco. They are brown and fit in your palm. Clouds like slivers float past without intercepting the clear sky. Below is a field of maize rimmed by a curving cement road. The birds peck at plants and pavement. They eat gravel and corn.

A flock, each a speck, lifts off the ground, so high they cannot be mistaken for the cloud of dust and fumes a truck leaves behind. One disappears. It is not its absence in the shape of the flock but the velocity at which it drops that makes it visible. The gun shot makes it audible.

It is compact when it falls but lands with wings outstretched. Piedad does not inspect the bloodied body. She counts the bones in the wings like they are ribs. White feathers adhere to the structure below. Do not flutter up and off the way they do when in flight.

It does not look like an animal. Something found under layers of dirt and dust in a field. Not a stone but a fossil. She knows it will rot and somehow seep into the earth. Buries it and places the thorn atop like a gravestone.

Everything regains stillness. The air does not move but hangs. Sweat ceases to drip from her hairline. In this white heat it is nearly impossible to see. Her ears buzz. She swipes at them with a tired flick of the wrist. Does not feel a little body fall.

A figure appears in the doorway of her home. It is Carmen. She does not wave or speak to Piedad. Just waits for the dazed child to spot her. Though her skin pulls when it stretches the girl smiles at her mother.

It is so dark and cool indoors all she can do is sleep.

The Face of a Dove

Alba stares at the chicken coop. It houses a scaled dove. A tiger-striped dog peers in through the diamond-shaped mesh bent into a square by soiled rags fastened to four wooden posts that resemble masticated meat. A tin roof.

The sun blazes above. The ceiling stores its heat. Its light filters at an angle through the walls. The wire rhombuses cast a crescent pattern on the floor and the bird that hovers above it on a wooden perch that traverses the cage, its silhouette.

Folded wings covered in coal-rimmed, white feathers. A red crust encircles a beady eye on either side of its tucked face. Its pink feet render it almost human. He does not see her see him. Remains vigilant of the periphery. The dog that encircles it.

The pale body at rest expands. Wingspan. The cage obstructs flight. Black claws curl around wire. Pushes head through the hole. The broadest width of its neck obstructs. Releases grip. Grows heavy. Slips out.

Not a dead weight. It soars to the ceiling that scorches the tips of its wings. Defeated by the absence of the sky. It does not fall but float to the branch that once protruded from a tree.

Alba sits on a fallen tree. Where upturned roots bend and bind into a single trunk. A hand rests on her wide stomach. Fingers flex and straighten caressing her cheek. She picks something off the ground.

Fits her fist in the cage. The bird does not fit in her palm. Drops a handful of pumpkin seeds on a metal plate. A sound. It flies to the rim, unafraid. Picks open the shells and ingests. She traces the rim of its feather with the tip of her nail.

Watching the dove eat bores her. As does watching it fly to the roof, try to fit through the holes, flutter down again. She studies its droppings instead. Size and shape vary. How it splatters depends on the height at which it excretes. All resemble islands from an aerial view.

She imagines walking into the sea. Sand burns the soles of her feet. A breaking wave dampens the cuff of her skirt. She waits for the tide to rise. It covers her knees and then where her legs begin. The dusty pink cloth that covers them floats up around her.

Falls onto her back. Waves carry her. Wash her hair clean. She turns so the sun reaches the back of her head. The salt stings her eyes. It turns the rims of her lids red. Her vision clouds. She cannot see the sky.

She recognizes a voice. Padre Pedro's booms: "¡*Vivimos en el jardín del Edén! ¡Canten! Gritan al cantar.*" (We live in the garden of Eden! Sing! Singing you can scream.) It streams through an open window from a radio on the kitchen table of the house next door.

The silhouette of a girl under the shadow of a tall columnar cactus by the side of the road. It is the neighbor's eldest daughter, Guadalupe. An outstretched hand inspects the stiff fruit protruding from an areola. The pink rind cracks open when it is ripe. They are green and tight.

The red flowers are in bloom. Tight petals enclose multiple stamens. She picks off a blossom and then the thorns off the stem. Places it on the now smooth surface with a piece of paper over it. Passes her pencil over the protruding surface. Its outline remains.

Drops the blossom. Stomps on it. Bends down to caress the now rough petals. They feel like her cheeks. The petals will never fall off and scatter. The bloom will remain whole. Buried. Places the imprint atop to mark the spot.

Returns to the plastic chair on the denuded lawn. Takes a round case from her pocket. It fits in her hand. The setting sun shines on the metal rim and reveals a protrusion. Pressing, it pops opens.

An enamel peony in her palm. A mirror facing her. Only her eyes fit in the frame. She meets her own gaze. It betrays fright. She caresses where her eyebrows meet. Guadalupe looks like a dove. No one notices but Alba.

Tiny Tombstones

Loose sand seals the holes in the hard dirt road. Pale, flesh-colored grains float like particles of air grown tangible. They hit a barrier and accumulate in mounds at the foot. Each grain, separate. They move in unison.

Inocencio watches them seep in under the heavy, wooden front door to his home. In the hollow space between those four walls it grows into a cloud. Fills the space within or between his possessions. This room is not empty.

A gray film coats his bed, television, and desk. Dust unlike sand is a nearly invisible lining. Run the fleshy underside of your finger across a tile to trace a line. Rubbing index against thumb feel the once dry substance turn sticky like the grease on your stove.

He sits on the floor before his low desk. A long plywood bench. Two piles of paper on either end. Scribbled on both are things he cannot forget. Those to his left are reminders, tasks. To his right, memories. What he does fills his days. What he remembers, his nights.

The slip in his hand flickers on a memory as vivid as the scene playing on the lit television behind him. A portable set like those in tollbooths. In the dark, the sun starting to burn through drawn curtains is still too dim, the screen floods the room with steel fluorescent light.

Past midnight the national TV station plays *La burrerita de Ypacaraí*. A large-breasted woman sits atop a donkey. Her lips and dress are the same shade of crimson and the sky is a phosphorescent blue. The film must have been black and white, then colored by hand.

"The day Belén died" is the sentence inscribed on that mnemonic slip. Smudges of lead where the pencil indented with intent. He remembers the facts but not her body or face. She remains fifteen years old and five foot, four inches tall.

He watched the girl wait. She stood by the bus stop before the only wall-enclosed home in Cayim ô Clim. It cast a shadow on the lawn within, rather than on her. The sun shined on her forehead like a bird fluttering in place. She did not seem to notice it because it did not shine in her eyes.

There was a bang. She turned to face incoming traffic. The noise came from within the brick structure she leaned on. Behind it stood a one-story home, a fountain that matched the stature of a girl, and a parked red car. The man in the front seat has just reversed into the wall.

Unlike lightning preceding thunder, the sound foreshadowed the fall. First the wall trembled and regained stillness. Then, it collapsed. The bricks fell forth, separating from each other; struck the sidewalk or something hard; and disintegrated.

Only the base remained. A barrier tall enough to bar the entrance of rodents and cockroaches. Mice can make themselves small enough to enter through a window slightly ajar, a pipe with one end in a ditch and the other in a tub, a crack in a wall.

The cloud of crumbled bricks and the cement between them settled. The home behind the three-inch-high barrier was exposed. As fragile as a house of popsicle sticks. The bars on the windows remained strong. They stripped the floral drapes of their joy.

The fountain ridiculed the pile of rubble. It endured. The statue's puckered mouth seeped water. Her thick arms still held the folding cloth that both covered and revealed her form. A moth stood on her big, hairless stone toe.

Water sprinkled on its opaque but nearly translucent wings. Anything could pierce the moistened frail material. Nothing did. Particles of cement clung to its wings, making them hard.

The debris-coated car concealed its occupant. Everything was still. He remained within.

The driver was not mourning the cost of rebuilding the wall. The door was jammed. He was squinting through the gray coating on the rear window.

Figures gathered on the sidewalk opposite his home. The words they uttered were unintelligible. Their faces indiscernible. Perhaps they were speechless, staring.

The first to arrive picked the girl from the rubble. Belén resembled a statue. Her clothes, hair, and flesh were covered in fragments of rock. Hers was a dead weight. But nimbler than stone.

One held her by the armpits. The other parted her legs to grasp her knees. Hands and feet dangled. Lower back and bum curved towards the floor. The mangled body swayed as they raced to the Mennonite hospital. More harm done on the way.

She did not grimace or wail with pain. Her eyes were large and her mouth, open. She seemed to see more and breathe deeper than before. "The face of a saint or an angel," her mother said. Not that of a girl who hugged and tugged at those she loved until they struck her still.

Her mother called her La Mimosa Arisca. Her siblings called her cowardly. She expressed affection persistently and spontaneously but winced when others reciprocated. The desire for touch got her in trouble. Her fear got her out. She foresaw and evaded others initiating touch.

She held the hand of the girl sitting beside her in class, combed back the hair of a disheveled neighbor, stroked the back of the hand of a stranger who rested it on the supermarket counter. They all peered back at her. Each time, she pulled away and ran.

Belén filled the cracks in the walls of her home with notes. After she died, they started to find them. Tugged on the diminutively folded pages by indenting index and thumb nail into the paper. With it emerged an exhale of dust.

The one for her sister read, "I love you though you are cruel when we are alone." Her brother's, "I love you though you ignore me at school and at home." The one dedicated to her mother was private. It read, "I love you most of all." She continued expressing affection and disabling reciprocation posthumously.

The crowd continued to gather before the collapsed wall. The corners of the bricks remained whole. The interior disintegrated into an inhalable powder. It stuck to the lining of their lungs. It covered the slim corpse before it was prised out of its mold.

They gathered to see the depression her body left in the rubble. Legs touching. Hands open by her hips. A tiny head. The wall crumbled on her hard bones. It killed her and took on her shape.

The bricks were old. Particles were compacted but did not adhere to each other. If struck with an axe the blade did not break and the stone did not part in two, it crumbled. With the blow of the car's steel bumper, propelled back by rolling wheels, they came apart.

Crumbled cement and fragments of burgundy bricks atop loose sand and compacted red soil. Those that pass the site of the accident stare. They match the color to the source. Cement and sand; soil and stone, do not match the brown and gray tones of their elements.

They make a red as deep as the black sea water far offshore. You do not feel the pull to fall when you peer in. As opaque as the ephemeral clouds that float away with sand and cement. You do not imagine shapes in the soil like you would in the sky. The first is tangible.

A child etched a storm onto the surface. Indenting his nail into the sand which adhered to the tip of his wet index. Revealed the compacted soil below. The rain was red. The air was brown. The air in his drawing was as thick as water the day Belén fell.

No one cleared the sidewalk. The wind swept away the loose cement. A thin new layer lined the now paler soil of Cayim ô Clim. Her mother stares at the ground when she walks and stalls at the site. The burgundy fragments remain. Tiny tombstones.

Inocencio peers down at the scattered pages. *The handwriting of a madman*, he thinks. Almost forgetting it is his own. He presses the pencil with such force the paper becomes liquid. Run your finger through spilt milk to see the wooden tabletop below.

His straight lines refuse to curve into legible symbols. His "b" is not a line with a half circle on the end. Replace the latter with a triangle. Sides do not meet at an angle. The space between them is charged.

Determined markings never intersect or touch and have no

outside. They fail to become the boundaries of an object. Occupy their own place in the boundless space of the page.

His children throw away his letters. Only he cannot cease trying to understand himself. The letters on the note he read were legible. The message, clear. The event, real. Still, he misremembered the perspective from which he observed the accident occur.

The dust that gathers on each of the four corners of his room gleams. Draws closer where wall meets wall. A translucent web over a stained, white pillow. The spider dangles from a strong, thin thread. He cannot see what hangs above him because he is looking ahead.

That intangible, gray matter lines the shelves that encircle the room. Few possessions propped on them. A tidy pile of worn, beige clothes. A cassette. Printed on a paper in the case: "*Una oración para la inocencia.*" (A prayer for innocence.) A photograph of himself when he was younger.

He wears a Paraguayan football jersey. There is a road behind him. The corner is tinted white by light. It is the sun's rays that flooded into the lens. In that image he is not in Cayim ô Clim but Pozo Colorado. He misses the music, traffic, and familiarity of Spanish spoken loudly.

He hears a rustle of feet and high-pitched but hushed voices. Approaches the window through which he saw Belén fall under the weight of the wall. He places his hand and forearm on the frame. It feels dry.

Traces the ledge with his index to wipe it clean. The dust adheres. He shakes it off. It does not fall to the ground but floats onto the wall. This film is charged with static. He runs his still unclean hand through his hair and feels the tips rise towards the ceiling.

The voices grow clearer. Children at play. One gives orders and the others feign distraction in order to disobey. Their bodies move quickly as they race. He hears their feet hit something wet. The squelching of soles as they disperse water to either side of a puddle.

He draws close to the glass. The sun is blazing now. Shades his eyes with his right hand. He sees the neighbor's children in his yard. Something is wrong. It is not just that the land is wet rather than dry. There is no barrier to intercept intruders or impede sight of the sidewalk.

His window was not opposite the external but internal face of the now absent wall. Through it he saw the red car race in reverse. Halt. Watched the barrier fall forth. He did not see the girl disappear. His was the only enclosed house.

He watched the people gather, carry the body, and remain hesitant to leave. Felt they would enter his home. The car windows were covered in debris. Feared his father would never emerge. He could see his silhouette still in the driver's seat.

Inocencio did not move. He was a child then. An adult now. Their home, this house, was filled with people once. Neighbors or relatives. Now he resides here alone. Unemployed but always occupied.

He sits back on the floor before his low desk. Takes a note from the pile to his left—a reminder. This slip of paper is longer than the rest but folded in half. It holds two sets of instructions: turn the fountain on *and* off.

Doors of adjacent homes start to knock open and closed. The sweat on the dark red flesh of the men that return for lunch dries and acquires a sheen indoors. There is a switch by the door of his home. It points up to signal something is on. The porch light is off. Water gushes from the statue's mouth.

It overflows from the basin under her feet onto the lawn. The expanse of white parched soil with patches of green grass has turned into a marsh. On its surface the latter float like lily pads. The yellow blades in the middle are the blossoms.

He flicks the switch down. A last drop falls like drool from her exaggeratedly full stone lips. The muddied water moistens his soles and his black plastic sandals make a soft sucking sound. He steps over the low barrier that was the wall.

Here the ground is as hard as pavement. Still it is not even. Irregular spheres where the land indents slightly. They resemble the water stains on untreated wood. Holes where rodents or lizards bury themselves, not to hide, but to cool themselves.

Inocencio's home lies at the intersection where the Mennonite colony becomes the Nivaklé settlement. Right and left men and women the size of grains of sand move on their own. Legs bend and feet alternate landing ahead of each other. Still the wind propels them back or forth.

On the opposite end of his block a group sits around a radio. It streams music but they refuse to stand and sway. They are not listening to the lyrics or to each other, none speak.

Their stillness allows them to see a cloud as ephemeral as an exhale in the clear sky, hear the exhaust of a car regurgitating fumes from an exhaust pipe, feel the relief of a flea-ridden dog when he rubs his pelt against the trunk of a thorn tree.

He tries to regain the calm he imagines that noticing things requires. Instead he feels discomfort. Something small and hard under his foot. Fragments of brick remain embedded in the hard soil. He does not kick them along the path. They may be the tips of buried boulders.

The thin hairs on the back of his upper arm stand rooted in protruding follicles. Swift changes become omens when he feels alone. The sky turns dark and the day cool. Still it does not look like rain. A windstorm.

If he remains still, the outline of his frame displaces the particles. If he moves, it seeps into his eyes and ears but pushes with force against his lifted leg. Space is a curtain. It molds to the body like a garment but the hand never finds the opening.

All the loose soil the wind displaces accumulates where the air is stale. Not a pile as high as the boulders but frailer. An imperceptible layer. Only the refusal of the loose particles to adhere to each other differentiates them from the hard earth or cement below.

A landscape of holes and protrusions remains where the wind blows. Next to a crater, a boulder. The height of the land above sea level varies. There is no flat surface, plateau, from which to measure.

He does not stray from his vantage point. Instead imagines climbing up the boulder. His ankles aching where they bend and his thighs burning. Toes pointing towards the sky but eyes anchored to the ground.

Descending into the crater feels like falling. Legs so loose that when he bends his knees they land on the soil. Instead of rolling or sliding down he remains in a crouching position. Open palms below his face impede his fall.

Peering at his hands he realizes that he can only see their outline. The light turned from blazing white to red and now pitch black.

It is not an eclipse but the setting sun. The wind has not blown away the sand revealing the hidden shape of the land. It has just grown dark.

The boulders are outlines of homes and the craters are the places where the thorn bushes grow. The latter are too far behind the homes from which light emanates. In the pitch black, what grows in the distance disappears like the base of holes in the ground.

Inocencio's nights become days and nights again while he misremembers the past. It disables him from straightening his sheets at dawn; preparing three meals; washing his pot, plate, and fork; and bathing at dusk.

He turns to the recent past instead. The children in the yard. How they disappeared before he stepped outdoors. He sees them around a round table through the window lit from within next door.

A woman that looks like Belén feeds them like chicks in a nest. She encircles them setting a sausage and slice of *sopa paraguaya* on the faces of the Disney characters that illustrate each plate. They prick the meat with their forks, carry it into their own open mouths, and ingest the chunk bitten off.

He wonders if instead of misremembering the past he is foreshadowing the future. He knows that Belén is not the mother but adolescent daughter next door. He remembers that she takes the bus to Filadelfia on weekends at midday. There she cleans the Klassen's home.

Perhaps one day a wall will topple her and after the wind spreads the rubble and ashes it will blow with enough force to lift all the sand and dust that fills the crevices between the real elevations and depressions of the earth's surface.

As he walks home in the dark, he stumbles on the barrier that was once the wall.

III.

La Paz del Chaco Street

Agatha

The dry, persistent sun and wind expunge the remnants of the family that fled La Paz del Chaco Street. A sound like soft rain if you bring your ear to the rubble of the Klassen's home. The gray mortar between red bricks crumbles out to mix with sand. A reminder that keeping a home whole is a constant chore.

Behind tinted windows, barren land and clear skies collapse into an impenetrable surface. Beyond it, sand floats off the ground to make the air tangible and visible. Within, fat women sit on heavy *quebracho* chairs. Children kneel at their feet. The families that remain are walled in by cold cement.

Agatha Klassen sits beside Estela Delgado, her stepmother. She holds her plush cheek in one hand. Strokes the roof of one foot with the toes of the other. Caresses the angel on the top shelf of the glass vitrine with her eyes. To keep from finding herself endearing, studies the lines on the porcelain hand that cradles the figurine's tilted head.

Estela is twenty-four. She wears her black hair to her bum and keeps an albino Afghan hound draped over her knees. Her husband's children look like cherubs. Always flushed from running after the dog. Its tail sweeps across their eyes before it turns the corner. Their eyes drip.

Estela

She is not Mennonite or Nivaklé, but Paraguayan. As a child, only her family lived on that block between Neuland and Cayim ô Clim. At fourteen, she married. Marcelo Escobar was loud and a soldier. She preferred obeying his demands over being privy to Mennonite men's whispers.

Marcelo took her to the military base in Pozo Colorado. It surprised her that the land there was not red but black. Standing by the side of the broad dirt road, her husband's friend explained, "See the oil dripping from the trucks? It soaks into the soils core. If they build a cement road, the earth will grow copper again."

They lived there in a small house. She planted cloth flowers in the barren lawn. From the kitchen window she watched vultures pick at the synthetic petals. They took the pink or turquoise shreds in their beaks up to the branches of the very real tree their claws clung to.

They did not tear at the clothes she hung out to dry, flower patterns in similar colors on her printed blouses. They rested on the line. One end tied to a hook that protruded from the wall. The other, the trunk. They weighed it down. The hems of his pants and her dresses were always soiled.

Each time she peered out they were perched at a vantage point from which she was visible. Still, the drapes remained open. She felt seen by those beady eyes. Marcelo had bought them. A Mickey Mouse print on one side and sun stains on the other. Gathered with the shoelaces missing from her shoes. Illustrations concealed between folds.

There was an older specimen that did not fly as high. Its bald head was red, not gray. The other birds tore live rats from its beak. Eventually it stopped hunting. Grew thin. Picked its feathers until its body and face matched.

While she was rubbing a stain out of her husband's shirt, it flew into the laundry room window. Its claws grasped the sill. Swayed left and right. Let out a hiss. And tilted back. A thud when it hit the ground inches below. It did not rise again. She decided to leave that day.

Estela called her mother and learned her father had passed. With that excuse, she returned home. Married life had become her. She wore dresses instead of leggings and let her long hair loose. Her mother refused to cut it.

The newspaper cutting of an elderly Tita Merello under the headline "*Se dice de mí*" (They Say of Me) remained plastered on her bedroom wall. When the tape dried and it fell to the tiled floor, she was hired as a clerk at El Paraíso bakery.

She smelled of the thin layer of flour that covered her skin and hair. It made her complexion even lighter than it had become from remaining indoors. She was the only resident of Cayim ô Clim that worked for the Mennonites. Her mother was proud.

With the hard sun in her eyes she blinded herself from seeing, not hearing, passersby. Catching a glimpse of the voluptuous figure behind the counter, they hissed, "She was caught stroking the hand of the owner's son when she was a child. Imagine what she does now."

Still plastic bags filled with puffed loaves were exchanged for bills. No one mentioned that Abraham Klassen's wife was dead. It was Karin Dyck's absence that allowed Estela to enter deeper into the structure that used to house store and home. Now the latter is a few blocks from the main avenue.

She stroked his daughter's hair before sleep and fed his sons. Agatha was six; Dirk, four; and Martin, one. The youngest trailed after her asking for milk. It is in the fridge by the lard she reminded him. He caressed her breasts when she held him, like a dog in heat.

While the father watched the news of a country far from the one he refused to call his own, she walked in the dark to that intersection where her parents' home stood.

One evening she did not leave. She has not slept elsewhere to this day, five years later. The eldest is now eleven, a young woman.

The drapes she draws over each mosquito-netted window were not chosen by her. Neither was the furniture or children's names. They belong to Karin. Everything must be starched and bleached. When the sun streams in, her eyes burn and her darkness grows luminescent.

She feigns tolerance with the children. Feels something between love and fear for them. Their deaths worry her more than her own. They make sitting on this chair in this room at midday on September 28th, 2016 matter. She ensures they are fed and do not stray outdoors when they play.

Karin

Their mother died in the Filadelfia hospital. She could see the cross from her window. It stands where the main avenue and Transchaco Highway meet. Ten meters tall. Built straight. Karin willed it to bend. The steel structure covered in bricks, plaster, and yellow paint still bows where the two lines intersect.

The inability to make anything last or anyone complete a job well are Paraguayan qualities. Peter Dyck believes God is present in man's resolution. The cross is proof of his daughter's determination.

Karin was always strong willed. She did not persist in requesting what she needed or desired. It was in her silence that they learned. She proved her strength through refusal. Anytime she beat her father, it was a feat he admired.

He traveled to supervise the clearing of a matted forest plot or the purchasing of pre-contact tribes by the New Tribes Mission. The American missionaries evangelize the most isolated communities around the world. She would refuse to excrete what she consumed to make him feel guilt for leaving her and selling those indigenous souls.

What she ate of the meals her mother prepared grew smaller and smaller. Upon his return, they would feast. The girl grown slim but full-bellied would plump up. She would not nibble on a bun from the basket but peel the crust and swallow the soft interior whole.

She learned to bake bread with her mother. They would pummel the dough atop loose flour until it would hold together in a mass that did not stick to their sweating hands but fall heavy on the wooden table. A cloud of white dust covered their white hands and pastel colored clothes.

The heat from the stove made her face redden while she watched the loaves expand under the oven light. She knew not to stick her finger in the still moist dough. When it browned, she extracted the tray and fanned them with an old newspaper until they were tepid and dry.

They made large raviolis filled with crumbly ricotta cheese and covered in cream that they served on porcelain platters.

Each took the set of silver spoons in one and the other hand and cupped as much cream as could fill a plate.

She spread ketchup on them because the tomatoes were never ripe enough. The preserved, sweet sauce mixed with the cream to make a soup that she drank like water. She called it cook's treat. Her mother scowled.

They had preserved guava with yoghurt for dessert. She spooned the syrup from the jar and mixed it with the milky substance. Everything she ate did not require teeth. Her own set remained sharp, not blunted, by never cutting through slabs of steak.

Once she bit her tongue. Her father was talking about the women under the trees. They were growing fat on strawberry yoghurt, food which is supple. Instead, they could eat the innumerable avocadoes that fell from the trees and smashed the hoods of cars.

They were hungry for sugar not something that filled and weighed them down. Karin knew because she always tried to feel like them. Her teeth cut through her own flesh. Her mouth filled with blood. It did not taste sweet but sour.

She finished the water in her cup in gulps. The more she drank, the more she bled. A translucent, red substance pooled in the empty glass. Her sister saw it. Remained speechless. Became as pale as the tablecloth, filthy with grease stains.

Her tongue healed the way the skin she ripped with those canines from her cuticles and the hair she pulled at the root from her scalp grew back.

Her mother and aunts said she was a nervous girl. Her father called her intelligent. This implied she was wasted speaking to the women. When Karin was eighteen, he ordered her to go to veterinary school in Asunción. She obeyed.

There, she lived in a big house with ten other girls from Menno and Fernheim. They dressed the same, studied veterinary medicine or agriculture, and rarely spoke.

During the day, they sat around the dining room summarizing the contents of their bound photocopies in their legal pads. At night, returned to their rooms.

Each had a wardrobe, bed, and bedside table with a lamp kept lit at night. A single possession differentiated each.

One had a guitar, she played well; another, a photograph of her mother; and Karin, a cat. The only live thing she could take with her from home. She would have preferred one of her siblings but Michael, named after the youngest, would have to do.

She stroked the cat until she fell asleep and it slipped out from under her still hand.

It could not be more unlike its human counterpart. Wriggled until it submitted and purred like the domesticated animal it knew it was. Tried to slip out cracked windows to mate with stray cats beyond the metal door and shard-rimmed walls. Never escaped.

Her brother did not seem to want to. He worked for her father. She worked *with* him.

The nervousness she experienced as a child subsided. Instead she meant everything she said and did. It was not what she did but how she did it that was under her control. She had a way of folding the bills in her wallet, correcting a man that misspoke, and noting her tasks for each day. After she passed away no one could decrypt her code.

No one dared defy her and when something went wrong, they resorted to her.

One day, a girl vomited on the bus. She had been begging for money. Now no one ignored her. Without a word the passengers turned to Karin. They did not recognize her assurance, but her whiteness.

Her back remained straight and eyes, unflinching. She ordered the bus to stop, the driver's companion to clean, and an older woman to hold the sick child. When all was sterilized and assuaged, they continued on their way.

Knowing best was exhausting. Yet by controlling others, she controlled herself. If exiled, she would rip her nails from their beds, pull her teeth from her gums, and bite the tip of her tongue so it parted like a snake's.

When she was educated and old enough to marry, she returned. Neuland felt larger than the city because she could wander unaccompanied. Roaming she found the parcel where her home would be built. Denuded except for the tall *aguacolla*. Between its stems, the abandoned web of a spider.

She married the man that owned El Paraíso bakery. The course of Abraham's life was decided the day she taught him to bake a loaf. They were children then. While she watched him knead the dough, he felt sure he could do two things well: spend time with her and make bread.

He was two years younger than her and uneducated. Yet made money faster than she could. It came from the fields where he grew the wheat used to make those white loaves, stalks of soy, and livestock that plowed through the grass that humans could not feed on.

Her husband watched men work in his fields and bakery. Her children learned little at school, but in three languages. She stood behind the counter and imagined the trucks on the Transchaco Highway passing before her eyes. A proximate dream.

El Paraíso looked out onto Neuland's main avenue. The driver of each car that traversed it was recognizable. Neighbors she had always known or the men that did business with them. Sometimes a dog, an older woman with a child, or a boy alone walked in or past.

She related these sightings to her husband, relatives, and friends. They did not interest her. She simply had no other novelty to share.

It was the livestock trucks she thought about the most.

Those fattened, soon to be flayed and dismembered, bodies wheezing in a wooden cage as large as her first home imagined what they were deprived of: water to moisten their thick tongues or space to lay on their sides and a slight breeze in the afternoon heat.

The Cattle Driver

The conductor thought about the sea. He saw it for the first time when he was forty-one. Remembered laying on the sand where the tide came in but never reached his face. The grains were not nearly as warm as the plastic now under his feet but looked like loose gold.

Nothing happened on that trip. He crossed the border, delivered his load, called his boss from a payphone, and walked from his parked truck to the ocean's shore. It was a weekday. The beach was empty.

He walked along the shoreline. Seawater and sweat wet the hem of his pants and the collar of his shirt. Sand stuck to the moistened cloth. Soles buried deeper into the loose sand with each step. He let the weight of his body slow him to a standstill.

That night, he stretched out on a bed in a room without windows under a fan that created a current of air as cool as his breath and fell asleep before his lids finished closing.

The hours he spent in that box with his foot on the petal and one hand on the wheel had led him there, a place he could return to whenever he grew tired of the monotony of a road that always grows narrower in the horizon but never ends.

When Estela stays in bed, she watches the children through the window. It looks out onto the vast grassless lawn delimited only on one side by the neighbors' rose garden. The only furnishings are a steel rainwater tank and a plastic chair.

As the wind picks up dirt, they become three silhouettes. As small as they are but without features and the distinction between torso, arms, and legs blurred. They roll on the ground. First the crown of the head touches the soil. Then, the nape, back, bum, and soles. Rise to standing.

Something mindless about how they repeat the movement, not

growing bored until they do. Its sole purpose is entertainment. Martin and Dirk laugh at Agatha. She performs as well as they do, but it matters more that her clothes and hair are matted with dirt.

It even coats her lashes. She is nearsighted but refuses to wear glasses. When the dog's hair or dry soil strokes her pupils, it worsens. She settles into this blindness like someone that refuses to swim because they can float.

Her agility makes up for her sight. Never trips or hesitates to move. Runs feeling the proximity of objects. Things possessed or built emanate the energy of their owners or makers, inches from where the inanimate mass begins.

Her strength comes from awareness and acceptance. She trusts the first more than the latter. After turning twelve, the boundaries change. She becomes cautious about when, not how, to act. If her father sees what she conceals, he will keep her indoors with Estela.

Agatha, like her mother, will always look like a child. Karin even resembled one in her casket. It is the fullness of their cheeks and the scattered look in their eyes. In the evasion of the gaze lies the secret. They never look at you so you can stare at them. What they see is their own.

The day a cloud covers the sun and a brief rainfall teases the quenched soil, the girl starts to menstruate. Thick, dark blood pours out from within and, like oil, does not mix with the water in the toilet bowl.

That stream shifts something within. Her curiosity becomes suspicion. She ceases racing her brothers to the uppermost branches of a tree and to the depths of the encroaching forest. She climbs to hide and runs to flee. Their taunting no longer feels affectionate.

At times, she is still. Stands apart from boys and men. When in doubt, grasps the hand of an unsuspecting woman, relative or neighbor, always older. Nothing helps. She feels ill at ease in the company of those she knows, no one is a stranger.

Only when alone on the road or in her room does she stop seeing the potential for cruelty in harmless gestures. Her father's large hand stroking Estela's white Afghan, her youngest brother picking out soil from under his toenails with a knife, the man on horseback peering in through the window.

In her room a toe becomes a toe and a hand, a hand. The memory of a gaze never ceases frightening her. Comfort seems repulsively false. The distance between her and the men she knows grows. It is out of respect. In order to see her best. She begins to see herself as they do.

Her possessions belong to a girl she neither wants to find endearing or pitiful but does. A wooden dollhouse with roofs too low to fit her dolls upright. An open notebook full of galloping horses. The thorn, not seed, of a *palo borracho* planted in a pot of dirt.

She still recognizes that girl's mannerisms in herself. Performs to eradicate them. Before a mirror, she relaxes her forehead and jaw. Her eyes glaze over. The simulation of passivity shames and reassures her. She wants to hear what others say, express nothing if she disagrees.

Once outside, her walks take her further than before. She walks from the time school ends until her father finds her. The later he sets out, the further she will be. Sand merges with the wind. She finds comfort in finding it hard to see. It makes her surroundings unfamiliar.

She wants to leave where she no longer belongs. Not seek a new home. She can feel the expanse of space as time passes and her life grows shorter.

Finding her becomes a nightly chore Abraham resents. He arrives home. Showers while his wife prepares dinner. The boys filter in through the front door and into their rooms. His daughter is always missing.

While his wife sets the table, he puts his shoes back on. Drives slowly with one eye on the rearview mirror and another on the view out the windshield. If an animal or child intercepts, he will feel the steel structure graze the body and halt before it goes under.

He always spots her from behind. When he pulls up beside her, she stops. The later he sets out, the further she will be. The first time it happened he cursed her. Now a silence has settled between them as they sit side by side. He never asks her why.

He does not try to convince her to return. She is willing. In exchange he is willing to understand this is not the same girl. This filthy, fidgeting, hate-filled child is like a homeless woman he takes pity on every night.

After she showers, sits at the table, and says her prayers in silence along with the others, all realize her presence does not burden them, but its absence or unrecognizability does. Sometimes she performs the younger version of herself for them.

They know there is nowhere else for her to go even if she flees. Everything is simple. Everything is easy. All that can be done is to endure. They will continue to seek and bring her back. She will continue to feign resemblance.

Estela does not believe in this. She watches the girl. She fills her mouth with morsels of bread and meat. Her little jaw macerates them and digests. Yet, she grows bonier every day. It is as though the food ingested does not suffice to supplant the energy spent keeping her body still.

Her skin seems to tremble while seated at the table. It is not anger towards what those around her say. She does not hear them. But towards her body, once whole, now visibly penetrable where she bleeds. She wants to feel impenetrable.

She cannot jump out of her own skin so instead she alters how her body moves, the thoughts and feelings it betrays. It is odd how the suppression of her desires makes her actions precise. The less she understands what she wants, the more she can will herself to become someone else.

She sees her. An old woman sitting on a root somewhere lukewarm where *ombús* grow. They resemble arms more than branches do. In her gathered arthritic hands, the same thorn of the *palo borracho* she had planted as a child. That night Agatha unearths it.

Animals frighten her now. A dog begins to follow her one day. The next it is joined by another. The following, by a pack. They do not emerge from homes or the bush but materialize when she peers back. Keep a distance. Do not desist if she throws rocks.

She plops down on the ground by the side of the road. The slimmest and slimiest yellow one approaches slowly with its head bowed nearly between its front legs. It expects her to throw a bone, it will turn to fetch, and leave her alone.

She feels an irrepressible languor. Does not seek something to throw or rise to her feet. She remains still. It comes closer.

Sharp breath through its open mouth. It nudges her arm with its snout, bends its neck, and rubs its forehead against her bicep.

She watches it with an illusion of distance that dissipates when she realizes that the reality of its proximity does not imply harm but care. It wants nothing from her but this proximity and the fullness of her attention.

This begins to show her there is no strength in endurance, repression, and detachment. The structures that keep people and the things that surround them apart are as artificial as her pretense.

The fear subsides. The languor remains. She allows the animal to express affection for her but expresses none in return. For now, it is enough to feel it. For the first time since she started to bleed, she recognizes the legs bent under her that carried her here.

When in the company of others, she now seeks an animal in the proximity. Not to pet but observe. They know they are being watched. Some acknowledge it with a gaze that disconcerts her to her core. Most respect her distance and impose their own.

One morning, Estela encircles the house. She is peering into the surrounding bush for animals that approach but never enter the open space. The boys run after the Afghan's tail, never grasping it. Agatha sits on the veranda.

The stepmother watches her study the long grass. From how her eyes dart she can tell the girl is searching for stray snakes that slither and lurk. It is not out of fear but curiosity. At that moment, she knows her stepdaughter has recovered herself.

She approaches her slowly. They are never alone. She is frightened the girl believes her body and desires are innately depraved. Most women in Neuland do. The girl is still. Peers up. She resembles a wet pigeon. Less beautiful than red-eyed and afraid.

"Would you like to stay in the cabin tonight, Agatha?" Estela asks the one that nods and leads her by the hand. They leave a note. Pack clothes, toiletries, and food. Walk past the boys. Crouch into the entangled bushes. Gaze at the floor instead of each other. Twigs break under their feet.

The small house enveloped in a fabric of bushes and trees belonged to Agatha's grandmother. They clean until nightfall. The girl gathers the dust and dirt into heaps until the wood paneled floor is visible. The woman scrubs the floor with a rag and water, takes the sheets off the furniture, washes them—they dry in an hour—and makes the bed.

They bathe in the dark water of a man-made lake. The prints of *taguas* leading to it are fresh. Agatha lets the blood seep through her underwear and jeans. Then, sits. The mud adheres and dries, concealing the red stain.

Between the matted branches of the thorn trees she sees a pair of yellow eyes. They betray fear, not desire. He meets her gaze. An impenetrable tranquility washes over them. Neither will betray the other's right to be there.

She knows his name, Tanuuj. He will return in a dream, in the future, when they need each other.

The girl and the women return to the hut. They start a fire and place a steel rack over it. Tear at overcooked slabs of meat with their hands. Agatha enjoys the fibrous texture. Her body demands the blood it lost. Animals sense the scent and approach. They do not hear but feel them close. A force that delimits the shack and keeps the inhabitants of the forest and town at a distance.

Agatha points the flashlight. Illuminates a mound of wild boars by the foot of a tree. They are piled atop each other but still.

Their snouts, high foreheads, and red eyes grow distinct as the light remains pointed at them. As red as the girl's blue eyes in photographs.

Before sleep, Agatha cradles an ivory boar figurine between her palm and chest. Its stiff little legs indent into her skin. They leave a mark, first red, then paler than her flesh. She feels trampled by the animal the tusk was ripped from.

She hammers a hole into its neck with a thin nail, through it threads a thin piece of leather, and ties the ends around her neck. The talisman does not ward off evil but reminds her of who she is. Someone like her can make the land, animals, and trees bend to her favor even if the sun, wind, and absence of rain castigate her for it.

The girl confides in her stepmother. She mistook the origin of the blood, the uterus shedding its lining, for an organ burst by a fall. Recalled the times she jumped from precipices or said things that made her father kick her off her chair. Felt lucky to die young, a slow and painless death.

Caring for her body is harder now. She must flatten her chest with a bra. Place and replace folded cotton where her underwear meets the space between her legs. If not, her body will exude a smell. Even if she does the scent emanates but subtler.

The stepmother explains why she menstruates, compares her to Mary. Then, the girl grows frightened and feels guilt. Mistakes not conceiving for conceiving immaculately and miscarrying the son of God.

The girl asks the woman if she ever lost a child. She says one never formed in her womb. When Abraham married her, she was too old. Agatha knows this is a lie. Estela is only twelve years older than her.

Something was forced into and torn from Estela's pubescent body. A blonde, dark-skinned boy her surrogate daughter's age. He belongs to his birth father and adoptive mother. She feels no desire for proximity to him. He was born without her consent.

Estela regained wholeness. Her lush flesh occupies space, her guttural laugh reverberates, and straight black hair flutters like a flag behind her. She feels pride for the ways her body calls attention to itself. Nothing is unconscious. The mouths of those that dislike her purse and their waists cinch for as long as they watch her, holding their breath.

Agatha is stiff. When she moves her body barely bends. The words she utters are unfelt. She chooses whose gaze to return. Caution strips her life of excess but makes up for it with the sureness of someone that walks away or responds with silence.

Everything in her life is based on refusal. She has nothing to say, nowhere to go. Still remains aware of how the passing of each day renders her older. An urgency builds. She does not fear the end of her days but a tear in time that will alter her memory of what anteceded.

After maintaining her gaze on Estela while seeing herself from the outside, she realizes the first is asleep. She is hunched in the plastic chair. The plate still on her lap. Her cheeks reddened though still dark from the blazing fire before her.

The girl picks the plate up and kicks dirt on the flame, extinguishing it. She feels older. Able to care for herself if she can care for another. While washing with a bucket of cold water in the tiled room with a squat toilet, she hears the woman enter.

The woman in the hard *quebracho* bed covered with a thin cotton sheet is asleep again. She seems more alive as her body fills and empties at a steady pace. Her brow furrows. The child never noticed it before. A wrinkle left of center between her eyebrows.

Agatha changes and uses the rest of the water to relieve the heat she feels her nape and back store. That night she dreams of a plausible future.

She is herself but older. Remains in this small dilapidated house. It is unlike her childhood home. Not shared with sons like her brothers and a husband like her father.

The branches of the trees and bushes continue to encroach upon the space around it. She trims them weekly. Weekly replaces a broom. Sweeps out the dirt that collects in mounds daily. Daily pulls a bucket of water from the well.

She sits in the dark, windowless room. Briefly, the room is cool. She watches the dirt start to seep in between the door and the frame like the warm exhale of a giant.

A man is seated on the porch. Watching her exit and enter. Tanuuj is not a stranger or her husband. He shares the name of the man her aunt ran away with—her gravestone is above an empty casket buried in the small Neuland graveyard.

The name Viola Dyck engraved in stone is growing faint but the brown arabesque tiles on the platform delineating the shape of the casket glisten and stink of cleaning products massaged in with a wet towel. The only time her grandfather does women's work.

Both his stepdaughter and daughter passed away before him. The first was Karin. She never knew the man whose last name followed her first was not her birthfather. The latter was Viola.

Some pity him. Others suspect he pushed them to endure too much. They committed to what could not be undone: a stranger and the river.

Peter Dyck turned Karin into a martyr. Yet she did not know that the river she tried to drown in was on the property the Brazilian cow herders want to purchase. She was not making them bend to her will but choosing to cease enduring.

Agatha sought a life in which stillness and action alternated in the daily chores and nightly rest of a life lived alone. It was the presence of men that disabled women from being alone in the evening after the work was done.

Her work would always be performed outdoors. Like the men, her skin grew tough and wrinkled. Her sight, impaired by halos from staring at the fields in flames. Her body, permanently marred by burnt red lines around biceps and legs.

The hardness of her bones proved she could do their work.

At dawn, she remembers thinking she was beautiful. Not the combination of pigeon and foal she resembles now. Doubts it was her after all. A dream is an alternate reality that can seep into this one as the dirt swept by the wind enters the home.

The life led on La Paz del Chaco continues without her. Her preadolescent self remains with her father and brother. The future and present blur when she refuses to return. Estela predicted this. Told no one. Returns home alone.

Abraham does not comment on the inevitable. They feel her absence and her proximity. He no longer has to search for her but can visit, he does not. He has achieved all he wanted—to know where she is. He knows she cannot leave. They are all alike.

Her life as a woman begins with feeling alone. Fearing the dark. Fixing the home. Leaving a light on so a passerby can tell the house is occupied from afar. The hours pass slowly though she works to exhaustion. Her father sends her a zebu to care for.

A Paraguayan man leads it there. Observes the red-faced woman barring his entrance with her body. Wonders why she would choose to inhabit a home the heat swelters into through netted windows like sweat pouring through pores. Instead, she could sit idly in the interior of a sealed home so dark and cool she would forget night becomes day. He leaves.

She is alone again. No one visits. The cow grows fatter, still its flesh clings off a skeleton. Its hanging stomach carries the weight, like an alcoholic man. The nights are longest. She watches the hours of the clock turn until it is late enough to get up.

Branches rustling with more force than a carefully pacing animal would exert wake her from sleep. It reaches the clearing and continues. She hears the steps grow muffled but louder as he steps onto the wood-paneled veranda. He sits with his back against the external side of the wall her head rests on.

The light is on. He knows someone sleeps within but feels relentlessly sure that nothing will occur if he comes into contact with her. She feels the languor that disabled her from moving when the dog approached. It is Tanuuj.

In their silence and lack of physical proximity she finds the peace of a life stripped of disappointment. Nothing happens. Each day resembles the next. Both are always there. Nothing more is shared.

He witnesses what she will not share: a reluctance to be still with herself. The dark circles under her eyes when she wakes from a sleepless night. The pain evidenced in her brow when she carries a heavy load. An anxiety that passes fleetingly like a specter before her eyes when the day's chores are done.

She lets her hair grow as long as Estela's. Wraps it around her head. Keeps it in place with pins, like needles. It does not come undone when she kneels and arches her neck to milk the cow, folds in half to make the bed she slept in, and allows the steam from the pot she cooks in to separate each strand.

Her body grows lean and straight from work. When her legs bend to hold her upper body or arms to lift an object, she feels the muscles build. Her core remains soft. Where her skin sags a little, below her belly button, lies the possibility of carrying another life within.

She stops eating meat again. Only carob flour, which she uses to make bread, and cactus fruit. Something dry and something wet, both soft. The *tagua* tooth figurine hanging from her neck reminds her of her own set. As her teeth grow sharp by refusing to bite into the fiber of an animal, so does her desire for a man.

Still she refuses the distant cousins that visit from time to time. Tanuuj senses their impending arrival. He strays as far into the woods as he can go but still find his way back. No one must mistake him for what he knows he is not. He does not protect her when they enter her home.

Agatha invites them in for water. They feel ill at ease seeing what has become ordinary for her. The tiled floor is not visible under layers of dirt that floats in where the door does not quite reach the frame. It is only the matted trees around the house that keeps the wind from dragging in more.

An *ombú* grows in the middle of the room. They do not know she will not allow it to break through the roof although it has torn apart the tiled floor. Every day she climbs a ladder that Tanuuj holds in place from below and trims the branches that are still slim as they have just sprouted from the thicker ones that bend below.

Sometimes she feels like the tree. Protected from the wind and watered but forced to bend. Nothing keeps her in place or pushes her forth. The only choice she had to make is to remain in Karin's hut. Only she inherits something from her mother. No one else wants it.

The only light that reaches the *ombú* filters through the tiny holes in the mosquito netting. No worms crawl among its roots. No birds craft nests in which they lay eggs on its branches. When its leaves fall, imitating the changes in season outdoors, they are swept into the bin.

She wonders why she cares for living things in the way that stifled her. It is only by restraining its growth that they can cohabit. If the roots broke more tiles to grow deeper and the branches, bricks to grow higher, the indoors would become outdoors.

She lies in bed at the end of the day to admire her work. Its trunk is still thick and its leaves, dark though the curved branches betray torture. They extend and then spiral back in as though resisting the desire to depart.

It inspires awe in the strangers that enter her home. She restrains, not refuses, its sylvan desires. A compromise. This part of her that forces preexisting life and makes logic of the infliction is inherited from her ancestors.

As she rests, she observes herself in the mirror above her bed. Bright, red cheeks; muscular but lean body extended and limp; and long, blond hair between her flesh and the sheet from her bum to the crown of her head.

She looks flushed while working. Her skin does not appear burned until she lies below her reflection at dusk. It never grows dark but cannot refuse the heat from leaving a mark. She presses her index fingerprint against her forehead. As the redness subsides a white blotch appears.

Around the hair follicles from which white strands sprout it is brighter than she can imagine or see for herself. It is as though the crown of her head took the brunt of the sun she could not face. Still the skin between her eyelashes swells red.

Agatha never wants to hide from the heat or sit still. Sometimes the man enters the matted forest to sit under the thorn branches of a bush. Crawling into the earth, he remains cool, still, asleep. The sound of his body seeping into the soil makes that of people aloft far and near, subside.

At dawn he watches her exit through the swinging door. A kettle of boiled water already hanging by the handle in her hand. She settles on the rim where the tiles meet the dirt. Fills the cup of yerba until it emits steam over the rim and then sucks on the silver straw.

There is nothing to stare at except what restricts her sight. She compensates for the encroaching weeds, animals, and insects by moving at an equally persistent but faster pace. It is as though she too is attempting to take over someone's land.

Sometimes her chores do not feign to have a practical purpose. When she finds tracks on the soil by chance, she lies by them awaiting the animal's return. Only the prospect of alerting them keeps her from jumping to her feet.

She finds stillness filming animals do what they do when she is absent.

The boars come to sip from the rim of the lake, liquid so turbid it is nearly as dark as their fur. Slowly immerse themselves in that tepid body, until their feet cannot touch the ground while keeping their heads above water. They slowly march up and out to find a patch in the shade where they pile those heavy bodies atop one another composing a mound.

It is the redness of their beady eyes and the furrowing of their brows that betrays their knowledge of the woman accompanying them. They do not approach her or leave any sooner but simply avoid the spot where she lies with less trepidation than spite.

Her body emanates a smell that will adhere to their pelts and keep others from seeking their company. For a woman to take up so much space is both satisfying and disturbing. As though that kind of respect cannot last.

She plans sightings too. Chooses a spot in the matted forest, burrows into the soil, and aims the lens of her Nikon camera. Then, waits. Ceases sleeping or feeling hunger and thirst. Until a peccary, an armadillo, or a tuco-tuco, a small rodent, materializes.

In the dark which the white light of her laptop fills, she rewatches the scenes of animals working. They take no pleasure in doing what they must. She is more like them than she is like Tanuuj.

He ignores the animals. Watches her. Studies her body the way she does theirs. Inspects his own too. Appreciates how it glistens when he sweats, watches his muscles flex and extend, feels the width of his gallant smile with his finger.

Pleasure burns through him when he sits in the sun, emerges

from the thorn forest bleeding but with an animal under his arm, or lies on the deck with his body so straight he does not seem asleep but in peace.

He inspects himself the way those that cannot escape their bodies do, the physically ill. Still everything he says or does is executed as intended. He controls the vessel. Even when he dreams, he does not see himself as others do but peers down at his body through his eyes.

In his dreams space is explored more deeply than in the reality he inhabits. There are spaces he can enter. A beehive, the places the Transchaco leads to, the cave where his father and mother hide, wait for his return.

What he sees tends to make him remember or prophesize something from future or past. He does not share these scenes with anyone because Agatha prefers him not to. So, he becomes an absent presence, distant though beside her.

There is nothing he wants more than to touch her. Then, run far from that house with the tree sprouting out of the roof. Never return. *There must be some pleasure in preserving this distance*, he thinks.

Agatha likes to feel insects, animals, and people close and at work around her. She recognizes when their habits change with the strange mixture of pride and surprise a mother feels when her son disobeys. *How can she mistake herself for Mother Nature?* Tanuuj asks himself. Sometimes she is a fool.

No one can match the speed at which she works. She is always starting something. As she completes a task her hands are at work on something new or her feet are approaching the place where she will deposit the artifact.

It is between starting and finishing that she is most herself. There is a simplicity with which she understands what must be done and does it. When she was two her mother handed her three strips of ribbon and watched her braid them. No one had taught her how.

Hundreds of braids of scrapped cloth are tied to the four poles of her grandmother's *quebracho* bedframe. When her dresses are worn as thin as carbon paper she tears them into strips. Fits each of the three ribbons over and under, so they always touch, and ties the loose ends.

From the tips she hangs things she finds in the forest: a *palo borracho* thorn she pierces so the cloth can slip through, a dry honeycomb with all the honey dried or sucked out, or a dry cactus flower. They surround and protect her without occupying space on a surface.

She started collecting things when her mother died, perhaps because her grandfather often listed the things they lost when they emigrated. While he recited, he stroked the shell he picked off the shore of a port where the ship docked.

In Russia, livestock was abandoned and so were the elderly, they are buried below their dwindled crops and demolished homes. In Paraguay, they purchased a green hell and turned it into an earthly paradise by force.

Karin had few things but cared for them well. She did the same for her children. Their shoes were always shined, clothes ironed, and hair wet, just washed. The help only scrubbed the floors and bathroom. She had time for them.

Thinking of Karin leads Agatha to Neuland. She returns weekly for provisions and Sunday dinner with her family. This time, she encircles what was her home. Estela watches her through the window. She peers into her unoccupied room. It looks the same, but the closet and drawers are empty.

She sits where the elevated porch ends and curves towards the grass. The outdoor sink to her right and the clothing line before her. Nothing is hung on the line. It stretches from the pipe, connected to the faucet from which the water streams, to a tree trunk opposite.

Her only memory of Karin is of her dresses, one white and one blue, the same model. When one was worn, the other was washed and dried. The blazing sun burnt the stains away. Stains of children's spit on her shoulders and milk on her chest.

She remembers the cut of the dress. It came down over her knees. The first three buttons were always undone. The neck folded back. Her collarbones protruded beautifully, like a necklace. A small silver cross where the sternum began.

Sitting where her feet do not reach the ground. Agatha remembers her mother's body. She realizes it is how she wants hers to grow to look. It was the cavity of her chest rather than her cleavage which she found beautiful.

As an adult, she feels her hard knees under her dress. It is white, a viscose blend with a zipper. Still her big bones make her beautiful in a way that a soft curving body would make her ashamed. And yet a part of her is.

She grabs the place where her stomach meets pubic hair. That flab of fat is always there. It is the least attractive part of her body. A man will touch her there to show he knows her, not as others see her, but as she is: a girl trying but failing to control how her body calls attention to itself.

Pulling her dress away where it folds when she sits. A breeze sweeps between the buttons and dries the sweat. Drying the drops that seep where her skin folds. Where limbs meet each other or her torso. Under her breast, her arms, and between her thighs.

Her stepmother emerges from the backdoor and waves but walks past into the encroaching matted forest. The girl's belly protrudes a little more each time she catches sight of that hard body. She first noticed it while she watched her make her way against the wind towards the family's home four weeks ago for dinner.

Now there is something soft about her. The way her hands fall on her lap. They seem to cup her lower abdomen. She looks like she fears something will happen to her. Like a rabid dog will rip through her dress and flesh. She is most afraid for someone else.

Today, like every other day, Estela searches the forest for freshly stomped branches, an indent large enough to fit an animal. Steps into that space and urinates. No one in her family's home or street can see her.

Other times she inspects the lawn for snakes. Its shape does not protrude over the blades. As the animal moves, the grass ripples. It is a movement distinct to when it is prickled by the wind.

Once she found a tiny viper. It tried to shrink and lengthen its way away from her. She caught it by the tail. Picking it up off the ground she realized it had two pairs of legs and a furry, white head. It seemed like a snake mated with its prey, a mouse. Her husband laughs when she tells this story.

She always finds a mystery to solve. Who left a shattered glass wrapped in paper hidden in the trash? Why did her husband take longer to walk home from work? What does the woman across the street by the window every day at midday search for? Perhaps she is just staring at the wind gathering dust or the sun scorching the dirt.

The last took her the longest to decipher. She watched her neighbor from different angles on alternate days. Stood vigil over the front door. Peered into the windows on either side of the home. No one except Greta ever entered or exited that house.

Greta

She turned bitter, cruel after her son left. Barely noticed when her husband passed away. From her threshold she explains to visitors that her prerogative now is not to simulate gratitude for their feigned kindness but to remain alone.

Nothing ever happened within that home. Only memories haunted her. Desperation for an ally, veiled as curiosity, led Estela to befriend the old woman. No one except her adopted family felt obliged to speak to her.

Weaving through the supermarket alleys Estela stares at the contents of her cart or the tiles under its wheels. In part because she fears the other women will peer back the way an animal does. Politeness ceases in silence.

She sees the curled-up toes of her neighbor. Yellow nails coated in pink varnish encrusted into plastic slip sandals. Plump but sagging legs covered in stray, white hairs. A patterned dress, flowers so small ten could fit on a bottle cap. Before reaching the neck, she feels those eyes set deep in their cavities grazing her own face.

The woman she has watched for so long in silence mutters a greeting with little emotion but more than anyone has expressed towards her in the past six years.

Something barely noticeable happens; the old woman sets her groceries in Estela's cart. They checkout and leave together. It is when they sit at the massive *quebracho* table, on which the woman eats all her meals alone, that things witnessed from one window to another collide with what occurs behind walls.

Greta has a son, Carl. He had a white horse called El Bicho that turned gray when covered with flies. They would traverse La Paz del Chaco Street from where it met a highway to the dead end. The horse's tail slapping away insects and picking up dirt. The boy propped atop the tall specimen like a tiny prince.

He pictured himself as the jockey in his favorite movie. A child actor played Mike in the beginning. They looked alike. The boy before the screen and the one within. A twenty-year-old film made for television. In it a child becomes a man when he runs away to the city.

There is a scene that lasts too long in which he rides the horse down a dirt road. It becomes paved suddenly and the surroundings transform. An island city-state of futuristic skyscrapers rises around him. It is unlike the mainland capital of Paraguay which curves around the Paraguay River and has low houses with baroque balconies and abandoned gardens.

If he did not have to pull on the horse's reins when the dirt met the pavement, a metropolis like the one from the movie would appear like a mirage in the heat. He always turned around because trucks race down the highway.

He heard them at night. The dirt gathered around the frame and on the floor directly below his bed is a trace of the gust of wind that swept through his open window but also of a stranger, the driver of the car that displaced the compacted dry soil.

After tracing the length of La Paz del Chaco Street five or six times he returned home. Sipped the hot cup of milk his mother prepared regardless of the heat. Bringing his face to the steaming surface his cheeks grew red. He was always sweating.

When he turned sixteen his uncle in Fernheim ordered him to travel the distance between the colonies on horseback to help harvest the peanut fields. By then Carl had forgotten about the jockey he thought he was destined to be.

As the stallion's hoofs hit the concrete floor something shifted within. Evil would occur that day. That night he was forced to gallop to a house he would recognize at dawn.

As the animal's legs bent and inched forth, he envisioned himself at different stages in his life as seen by another.

At six, sitting before the old television set with his back and neck curved so his head rested on his hands without pushing against his jaw because his mouth remained agape.

At twelve, returning from riding with an appetite that led him to move fast and speak rashly. Sitting at the table he would demand milk, bread, and cheese. Greta would take her time to hear him whine, still a child.

That morning, at sixteen, riding off with the bag strapped onto the horse's back. The sun shining on his own back with such force that the white shirt grew transparent where it clung to his wet skin though he had only emerged from his cool, dark home minutes earlier. Salty beads seeped into his eyes from where his hairline began.

It was midday and the sun shined brighter than hours before.
He stopped sweating. From that day on he never did again.
His body chose to retain everything and refused to produce
waste. Noticing his forehead was dry as he ran his hand across
it, he chose to stop remembering.

He made a life for himself in Filadelfia. Lived with his uncle
until he had enough money to buy his own home, smaller
but nearby. Married a woman that looked like his mother
when she was young. Though distant, still a cousin.

Greta sits and watches the road disaffectedly waiting for his
return. Her memory lags. Sometimes she forgets how long
has passed since he left or she visited. Does not understand
why a child answers when she calls. Mistakes him for the
character in the film he loved.

Wonders if he will return victorious at forty on a horse like
the one he left on. Tie the animal to the steel rod in the
backyard. Climb the steps into the house, walk to his room,
and sit on his twin bed. Before him, a drawing of a house in
a field with smoke rising from the chimney. On his lap, an
album of images collected for her sake.

This is only a vivid dream that assuages her desires. He has
grown into a normal man, like the one she married, loyal to
his wife and offspring. She is the one that rewatches the film
to remember him as he was and imagine an adult version of
him.

Estela listens to all this while holding Greta's hand. The
gesture does not betray what she thinks. This woman, like
those whose gazes she avoids in the supermarket, lives in a

delusion of who her son is and husband was. She indulges Greta, does not say that Carl has outgrown her and that she suspects he is not that loyal to his children or wife.

There is a softness to the alternate realities these women create. They remind her of the miniature paintings that adorn every child's room in the colonies.

A Painting

One depicts a boy and a lush yet controlled landscape in which something small, a rolling ball with a dog running after it, is set in motion. These images conjure stories in which surprises are small and dependent on human cruelty and animating the inanimate.

The bushes that line the road on either side feel like soft cushions but restrain the passerby or animal from straying. This house though it emits warm light and you can imagine it filled with old but comfortable furniture has small windows you cannot peer through.

This boy despite being small and endearing—he has tiny hands and feet, flushed cheeks, and shorts that reveal pudgy knees—is missing a face. His featureless yet coifed head expresses no emotion as he watches his canine friend approach.

Their lives continue beyond the frame. The dog bites the hem of his pants. The boy, though sweet, grows frightened and kicks it in the throat. It falls onto its back. It looks the way it does when it scratches itself with the tough grass or wants him to rub its warm belly. He feels regret but has done it before.

This time it does not flip onto its side, stomach, and feet, running off to return at night. It remains unmoving. The boy worries until he makes up his mind to bury the dog, dead or alive. Placing a loafer-clad foot atop a mound to compress the dirt that covers the hole in which the body lies, still moving slightly.

He arrives home for dinner. Not sweat, dirt, or blood stained, but a bit wrinkled. He sits at the table and says, "Pucho ran away." "He'll return," his mother answers. She wants to ask: "Why?" He does not respond.

All the adult women in Neuland, stare at paintings, watch daytime television, or read novels that summon stories like this one. The desire for depictions of violence ensues from heat exhaustion or being forced to remain indoors to avoid it while others go to school or work.

All dream of someone like them elsewhere. They want something to happen without disturbing that structure that is not a semblance but foundation for each action they enact or thought they partake in throughout the day.

Estela's work as a sleuth was to discover what pitiful dreams they made up while they stood pensively by a window or laid out on their beds before crouching to scrub and then check a chore off a list.

Before crossing the street and entering her own home, Estela feels the wind blow her left and lets it lead her to the dead end. It pushes against her back, so her feet lift and step, a body propelled forth by another force than the soul.

In the vacant space between the sparse trees before the forest starts, sit men and women on plastic chairs or on the floor, all around a radio with its antenna pointing up. The sound that booms from it is not a song but a sermon.

Faces with thick lips are pressed against each other, their slits for eyes stare into space as though seeking and failing to pair the voice with something they can see, and the bodies fidget because what the faceless and bodiless man says is the most unsettling thing you can imagine.

The women have long skirts under which they conceal their filthy feet, and fleece jackets or old sweaters that belonged to someone that enjoyed sports and cuddling on a couch before a television screen.

The men wear slacks whose hems are frayed and fabric thinned by their bent and laboring bodies. Their labor buys the bread into which they sink their teeth. Even in repose their backs are straight and the caps or hats that once belonged to other men conceal something of each face.

The Nivaklé spend their days sitting, waiting. Not speaking, carrying out chores repeated daily or caring for children. None cradled on a lap or in a bed the right size. The small ones crawling, led by the warm wind. The older concealed behind something, a tree, doing what they would have been instructed not to do if their parents still spoke. Everything is silent. Not even the dogs howl anymore.

The evangelical pastor, Padre Pedro, describes a dystopic future.

A Sermon

The sky will refuse to seep water. The land will grow as hard as stone. Animals will bury themselves the way only reptiles do but will not reemerge to seek prey. The homes humans live in will be stripped of walls and ceilings, so torn cloth will be draped over what is left of the structures and it will not protect them from the heat of the sun or the cool of moonlit nights.

Dogs and horses will lay on their sides, their ribs separating and coming together as they gasp for air; doves and chickens will burrow into the soil until their slim necks give in and their heads meet their chests; rats and mosquitos will disappear, the first buried under fallen bricks and the latter incinerated by the sun.

Though life will be extinguished, a smell and sound will grow stronger and inescapable. It will be provoked by a fire still miles away burning through fields and homes, flesh of animals and humans. Leaving only the stone-hard ground, until the earth shakes.

At this point the voice in crescendo stalled and the radio clicked off. Before words merge with static and are subsumed by silence, Padre Pedro offers comfort in a warning: *"Esto es el infierno. No pases el más allá acá."* (This is hell. Do not spend your afterlife here.)

A woman responds, *"Mejor infierno conocido que por venir."* (Choose a familiar hell over the one to come.) She speaks softly but more sternly than the one whose voice propels to fill space. Those listening, including Estela, soak up the words like stale bread used to clean the oil off a plate. Not a gluttonous gesture but a refusal to waste.

They saw her approach and stall before them. She imagines herself in a parked car with the ignition still on. Feels ready to turn away. While she walks, she calculates that her husband and stepsons are pulling into the driveway right about now.

The groceries still hanging from her tired arms bang against her legs.

They do not expend time as quickly at night. Her stepsons are in their rooms. Each lifts a weight carried earlier in the day off his body as he falls onto his bed. Her husband is in the bathroom. He rinses the soil mixed with sweat from his flesh like from a cloth.

A chicken goes in the oven and before midnight they eat. While the skin turns into a brined crust, she watches her white dog glare at the gray dove in its cage. Such a small animal beside an elongated one. His muzzle reaches the tiny, wooden door.

One in its cage with a floor and roof of sticks set at such a distance that the inhabitant cannot fit through and must fly within the confines. The other in a tiled and wood paneled home in which it only fits if it remains in repose.

There is something narcissistically submissive about her pets. How they accept domestication in exchange for being admired.

Only she watches them. The others avoid the space the animals occupy. They believe keeping a distance from another body suffices as recognition that the other is alive. She thinks of the life she recognized in her stepdaughter earlier that day. Says nothing. Feels it grow each day.

Upon returning to the shack, Agatha showers using the water boiled and filled in the bucket above her head which she tilts slightly by pulling on a rope attached to a hole in the rim. Lathering soap on her stomach she feels the strange, firm roundness—not soft, like fat.

What she is starting to know is never spoken or fully formulated as a thought. It acquires tangible qualities slowly, like a premonition coming true. The imagined scene fades as the actor's needs intercept. Before it is real, it must play to the end.

Every night she ties ropes around the front and back doors' internal handles which stand at opposite sides of the windowless room. Ties the other ends to the thick trunk of the *ombú* in the middle of the room. The tree will not be uprooted by someone pulling on the external handle.

There are also locks on the doors on opposite sides of the house. She remembers while falling asleep. *Are they locked?* She gets up to place the key in each hole and turn. Doubts the strength of the ropes, if someone picks the lock and pulls the knob.

It is exhausting to guard her body and home so much. She is more like a woman that spends all day caring for the shape of her body, the feeling of her skin, or the length of her hair that coats it which must be ripped at the root, than she likes to accept. The difference is that she never doubts that she is a source of longing.

Impeding a man from fulfilling that desire is what will enable her to grow old. This is what she has wanted since she began to menstruate. The dehydrated appearance of flesh of the vagina resembles the drying from within of a wrinkled body that nears death. The end and beginning of life are felt where a woman can be penetrated.

The presence of the man outside is a security. It is exhausting to consider him another kind of threat. She does not.

During the day a breeze flows through both open doors. He waits on the porch for her to return at night when the chores are done. Not hiding but refusing to leave. Who could make him? She could. Only by agreeing to return to Neuland and marry.

She considers nailing the ropes to the front and back doors, which open out. Lying on her bed in the middle of the room. And tying the opposite ends to her left arm and right leg. This way she would feel the intruder. If he managed to enter, he would find a dismembered, already violated body.

Agatha pushes her head against the *quebracho* bedframe pressed against the wall. Those cement covered bricks push back with the force of a man's hand. It feels like the weight of a father's hand resting on his daughter's head. He whispers truthfully, "Nothing will happen to you."

Above, the white vermiculite ceiling. The tiny protrusions like rocks are still visible in the dark. A horizontal plane high above her outstretched body that does not encroach but protect. Below it, the bed, desk, and chair, her clothes for the next day folded neatly over the back.

Everything is still inside. She lies on her back. Her chest rises and falls with even breath. Calm in the night of a still life. It is the upkeep of the grounds and the home that make enough to eat and drink, keep the roof over her head from caving and the walls from giving in.

The wind sweeps over her dry roof. It tries to rip the thin, cascading bricks from where they fit together. The trunk of the tree within her home continues to be swayed like a body by waves. Something in the air sounds like a song. It is the wind.

It is not the birds that have forgotten how to sing and hide in holes in a trunk to be torn down. Not the snorts from boars' snouts which crevice between bodies piled atop each other as though they are not heavy enough to remain grounded. Not the wandering horse that nickers to the mare but was ridden so far from her it is not audible.

The sound of the wind as it moves between things which only the stale air kept apart. The space between bricks, branches, and the body of the man, Tanuuj. His back still lies against the opposite side of the same wall on which the head of Agatha's bed frame rests.

She feels him, does not hear or see him, somehow the weight of his back against the crown of her head is not impeded by the wall. They live like this. Always in each other's felt absence.

He guards her from those that are watching him. They are not predators with manes slicked by sweat hidden in the woods or crouching below the thin branches that spear out from the bushes with thorns.

They are men with flesh that indents when a hand presses against it. They sit behind the wheel of a car waiting for his absence and to accuse him of something untrue: sleeping with a woman against her will.

His legs outstretched on the floor before him. He sleeps sitting. Not curled into a ball as he did as a child. His mother would pull his legs out from under him and make him stretch out his arms like Christ on the cross. Instructing him to initiate, not protect himself from, an offense.

Letting the body occupy the space it does already makes him bigger. Still he is always stiff. Awake even when he is asleep. The first is truer than the latter. He can remain alert while others sleep because no energy is wastefully expended.

As a child his mother stitched two white feathers to a leather belt which she buckled over his bare chest. It made him beautifully pathetic, like a bird who plucks its wings and torso but cannot reach those on its back.

Tanuuj

He was a slight boy. The rest left him behind because they assumed he would die. Climbing up the highest tree to the sturdiest branch he scanned the forest for the clearing where the children played. So many boys running in the dirt they lifted off the ground with their heels.

Always a single figure with fast legs that led the pack. The rest followed, overexcited, tripping the ones ahead instead of gathering speed. Children that want to become men do not wait to grow older, they prove themselves.

The one that led the rest was not easily identifiable when they returned. Not the short, sturdy boy that pummeled anyone that outdid him. The one with his shins bruised or bleeding upon their return. After the run the boys left him behind too.

Tanuuj climbed down and approached the one apart from the rest. Grabbed a handful of soil and patted it onto the scrape to turn the blood dry. At first his new friend, Casamshi, cringed. Then, the muscles of his face unclenched and the seeping from his knee stopped.

The next day, Tanuuj joined the race. He and Casamshi outran the rest. They reached a palm island. No vegetation within a twenty-meter circumference of a palm tree. One leaf kept both their bodies in the shade.

In the stillness of the heat everything remained in its place. Even a drop of sweat dried before it had the chance to drip down a face, neck, and chest.

There they catapulted themselves forth in time. Seeing all that they would endure until death, they felt resilient and mortal.

They did not return to where their families lived in homes made of tarp and string around fallen branches. Remained together, moving, and out of others' reach.

The shift they both felt was not stated but performed through touch. Tanuuj and Casamshi became lovers. They were closer to each other than either would ever be to a woman.

They started to hunt the cows that calmly fed on small patches of yellow grass which Peter Dyck and his sons worked so hard to grow. One disappeared and the carcass was found weeks later picked to the bone, by human fingers.

Peter drove past the two men always on the move. Noticed their jaws made strong by ripping into meat. Slowed down to make his presence, accusation, and impending retribution felt.

Soon after the man that outran the rest as a boy disappeared. Tanuuj knew Peter had taken his lifeless body to the palm island where they foresaw the future.

He stepped out of his shoes and onto the scorching sand that coats the red earth. Made his way home from memory. Slowly because this was all he could and had to do.

His soles grew blistered until those popped and seeped their yellow liquid into the thirsty earth and the newborn skin grew raw. In this rawness he felt a release. Like realizing you are crying upon touching your wet cheek.

Where the bushes' branches reaching left by the side of the road ceased in midair the opening grew with the space the roots of the palm made for itself underground. Nearing the shade offered by its large leaf he saw there something unburied.

Casamshi's carcass picked to the bone to render it unidentifiable. *My beloved is a beautiful corpse,* Tanuuj thought. A collection of ivory bones like the tusks of an elephant.

Tonight, while Agatha sleeps, he remembers his friend's face and body, how it moved when he ran. The voice that streams softly from the radio reminds him of Casamshi's. It belongs to someone in the choir that offers a sung response to the preacher's instructions.

He always knew he would lose Casamshi. Never imagined he would gain the granddaughter of the man that took him. He met Agatha in the matted forest the day Estela brought her to bleed in the river. He saw them from afar but did not approach.

Something in him began to change that day by the man-made lake as it had in the palm island years earlier. He felt companionship in her gaze. She saw him the way he saw through her. Something beyond touch occurred at a distance, a distance both maintain.

He lives with her. Not like a husband, brother, or son. Nor like a friend that leaves after a visit regardless of how long it lasts or how frequently it recurs. He cares for her in a way not even a mother can.

The distance they keep is set so others cannot push them further apart. It creates a force field around them which those men, familiar to her and recognizable to him, cannot cross.

They do few things to alter the abandoned forest that surrounds the lone shack beyond the lawn. Karin left the plot to Agatha. They are isolated because the soil there is stiff. The peanut and soy fields that begin beyond what the trees conceal are irrigated by water pumped from underground.

Still they pick the seeds from the fruit of the *palo borracho* that casts shade over the house. They fall on the roof like rocks that burst open. Large, black seeds coddled in beige cotton beneath the thick, green rind. Knocking the fruit against the rock-solid soil they pop one out at a time.

Dig with knives and forks into the ground. In each hole a seed is deposited. Agatha prises a floorboard from the living room and drops a seed. As the years pass *palo borrachos* grow to encircle the house. An *ombú* grows within.

They do not guard them from prying eyes because the entrance to the house is still visible between the swollen trunks. But they do shield them from the wind and dust. The rising branches like antennas give them something to follow into the always clear skies.

Never does a cloud appear. If one does, it comes adhered to others creating a menacing, dark mass overhead. Tanuuj does not enter the house but the forest. The canopy shields him from the rain. He feels the hardness of the bark though wet and the soil that remains compact despite the flood.

The house is hers, but she starts to go out to him. She grows older and the distance between them, smaller. He begins to enter the yard, the porch, and one day she finds him seated beside her, indoors.

They share meals; speak softly to each other in a language neither knows well, Spanish; and look at the same things for hours, taking turns to describe them. Not stories of events imagined. Renditions of nonhuman animacy.

A snail crawling into its shell, a boar's footpath wet but growing drier with the sun, the light of a passing car at a distance emanating like the sun until it grows dim the way the night arrives slowly.

The snail curled into itself, seeks shelter. Carries the burden of its shell. Gains traction by coiling and uncoiling. Despite appearances, it is not still.

Tanuuj reaches out to pick the snail off the ground. Something changes in them again. They witness how their presence is not ignored but noticed and felt intrusive to what surrounds them.

He smudges the black marks of soil left on the cement with his hands, kneeling. She fixes branches she broke to fit through the path by making them occupy the same space. Leaving things as they are, allows them to stay put.

He knows how he will die. Asks her if she wants to know. She answers no. What he gains from her and she takes from him is a desire to see everything that surrounds them before death.

Each day they rise before sunrise. Sit on the porch cross-legged. Watch the sun appear, become red, bright. She watches the outline of the bushes grow clear until she can tell the branches apart. He watches the outline of the house grow distinguished from the sky and canopies behind it, which it meshes into in the dark.

There is a certainty gained in telling things apart. It allows them to feel close while distinct. He watches her hand on her lap. She watches his fingers between the hairs that grow from the crook in his neck holding the bottom of the skull in place.

How they keep themselves upright and wake up each day is their own business but interest in the other allows them to lose track of themselves. Too much self-awareness would make them unable to bend their outstretched legs to standing.

That is the danger they impede by meeting, stillness. Their movements are slower than that of the dirt impelled by the wind, more careful than others, nearly in sync with each other's. Still they wake, eat, work, sleep, and wake to the next day.

A single task takes all day. Filling a bucket, soaking, and scrubbing their clothing until the collected water turns brown. Rinsing and wringing them until the water that seeps out is translucent. Strapping one end of a rope to a tree and the other to a column that helps hold the roof over the porch. Watching their hung garments dry.

He wears faded pink, blue, and yellow nylon shirts and pants. She wears blue and white dresses. The garments fill with air as if worn by phantom bodies.

He pictures strangers in American shopping malls purchasing replacements for the barely worn clothes they place in plastic bags, loaded onto trucks, shipped in containers, unloaded onto trucks, and dropped at the door of the Mennonite charity shop in Asunción.

She pictures Karin. Her clothes are cut from the mold her mother used. They have the same build, never at the same time. The waists of her dresses are growing tight. They reveal too much. Observing the translucency of the worn white garments, she excuses the expense for new cloth.

Tanuuj feels that only his body belongs to him. Agatha feels that everything, except the choices she makes, belongs to her family. He dresses in others' clothes. She washes a body that still belongs to the woman that gave birth to her.

He protects her from someone that will turn her body on all sides and bend it to see it from different angles. *This is mistreatment*, he thinks. He watches a child flicking an ant onto its back, its side, back onto its frail, now broken, legs. Without touching, only looking, this movement can be produced.

He waits on the corner of La Perdiz Street and the main avenue while Agatha buys cloth. Before him sits the boy with the ant. On the opposite corner, a man under the shadow of a tree on a white, plastic chair with a dog at his feet and his face reddened where the leaves do not touch. Agatha walks towards them down the nearly empty avenue.

Tanuuj tries to watch her the way the white man does.

He notices how her knees bend, the dress adheres to her gut, the sternum protrudes like a precious stone. His eyes never rise to meet her burning gaze but glazes over it to watch her white hair shine in the sun. He does not see the threat in the strangeness of her beauty.

This man sees Tanuuj watch her being watched. Imagines him grabbing the steel rod by his side and lunging towards him. While imagining this violent attack, he holds her still with his gaze. He does not want to possess her. And yet believes she belongs there, with them.

Trying to convince her of this is impossible. Even as a girl, she wandered too far. Down La Paz del Chaco to where neither children nor adults sought to enter. Into the matted forest or down the highway to nowhere in particular. A dog always followed her.

The underfed yellow ones that seem part hyena. They never fight but sometimes show their teeth. Canines reach over lips yet protrude only slightly from inflamed gums. Throw them a slab of meat and they will suck on it or nibble at best.

They roam in packs. Find a human to lead them. Often a young girl. Follow her to the store, a friend's home, her own. Wait outside the door until she emerges or desist and wander off.

Agatha led them so far astray they did not know how to return. Once she nearly reached Filadelfia. Another time she found herself in a clearing near where her grandmother built the first home in Neuland. The last time she wandered around Cayim ô Clim, the Nivaklé settlement named after a mythical hummingbird, which remains only three blocks from her parents' house.

The homes were made of tarp and broken branches that pushed from the ground like miniature trunks. From the outside, shadows lit by dying bonfires or voices in the dark. Within, bodies lying on the floor or on hanging hammocks, sleeping or speaking.

No one greeted her. She belonged here less than elsewhere. So, wanted to stay. It is in her nature to intrude. After all, she is the progeny of her grandmother and mother. Where no one dared enter, they did. She approached the deserted plaza at the center.

Even in the dark the outline of the blue hummingbird atop the cement platform was discernible. She brought her hand to touch it like she would pet a pony. Slowly caressing the cement. The surface was porous, like her face. It expanded. The pores grew large enough to fit her finger in.

A Statue

She wondered if it had been a runaway like her once. First, turned into a hummingbird. Not flying from flower to flower, but from the past to the future, bringing news of the afterlife to the living. Then, into stone to make her remain where she belonged, the present.

The men accused the flowers of petrifying the bird. They withered, without reproducing. Its long tongue with a slit in it was meant to suck nectar. Pollen from the stamens of one bloom was made to adhere to its small head and then the stigma of another. In its absence, they grew dry and ceased producing pollen or nectar.

A man grasped the hummingbird midflight. Its wings folded against its body like sheets of paper. Another held its beak shut like you would a venomous snake. The harmless bird was still but its heart still pumped blood, so its body shook.

While held in the palm it grew bloated. Larger and larger until he had to hold it with both hands. Then, it grew too heavy, so he dropped it. It was huge when it stopped growing. As big as a cow with its legs curled against its stomach. It was cold and as heavy as the stone it was now made of.

No one could pick it up. They made a cement platform beside it. Only able to push the stiff body onto it. Never able to lift. This is where it still lies. Agatha never repeated the story she made up while stroking the Cayim ô Clim mascot.

Her father found her curled between the bird's legs. She was not crying but keeping it company. It was Agatha, if she was an animal turned to stone. Her father was angry. So were the men and women in the surrounding homes. The children were curious.

She never crawled into the forest and for that he was thankful. He never chastised her because a part of him knew this was all she could do to survive. She had to move to remember she could. Would not leave the community she despised. Only test the boundaries of its territory.

A dog trails after her and Tanuuj as they walk home from the colony. His owner does not whistle. The dog does not peer back and return. The man rises and follows his pet. The ones that lead do not need to turn around to witness this slow chase. Nothing feels more real.

Its owner, Mark, who watched her earlier, is neither her relative nor neighbor. Still she knows what his sister looks like in a nightgown. He played with her brothers until the games were substituted with work and talk or drink.

While he follows them, he remembers her alone. Sitting in an empty classroom at midday. Refusing to play or speak incessantly. Patiently waiting for the day to end. Awaiting adulthood. She did not seek attention by leaving, just ran out of patience with being a child.

He resembles his father as much as his son resembles him. All live like their ancestors. Though they swapped the tundra for the desert. All share intimacies.

He remembers more about her than she knows. Everyone recalls the lights of her father's truck at dawn. Seeing the small figure beside him. They did not return to bed. Knew he picked her up in Cayim ô Clim.

Mark knows what led her to wander that day. She was not fleeing but questioning the borders between the segregated territories. It frightens him still. Makes him want to frighten her.

She is like her grandfather. Looks like her mother too. They led.

She can make a home where she is not welcome. Pushes the desire to belong out of herself. Along with her longing for a child.

Agatha knows where he lives. On La Guerra del Chaco, a street perpendicular to La Perdiz and parallel to La Paz del Chaco. They turn onto the second. Then, the latter. She feels disoriented when she knows where she is.

Stops before her parents' home. Tanuuj stops behind her. He is not quite still. Shifts his weight from leg to leg. Wasting energy rids him of anguish. The dog sits and the man beside him caresses his head.

Ten meters from the road. A green lawn between them. A single orange tree. It grows freely. The tank rises from the backyard. Water pumped into the hose moistens the soil below the tree. It never bears fruit. Comestible white flowers now bloom in bunches between its leaves.

It is a chalet. Red brick roof peeking over the encircling porch. Plastic mimicking rough stone covers the external walls. The same tinted windows that line storefronts and adjacent homes. Slabs of rock trace a winding path to the large double doors.

This is the house children imagine when they draw.

She tries to see her family within. The tinted windows are mirrors. Still she can remember their things and the feeling of being indoors.

The dark interior, cold bricks, and hard wood. A feeling of emptiness. The tiny things in vitrines. An arrowhead, the lace from the cuffs of her great grandmother's dress, and a note from her, it is illegible. Her own little room. The white quilt tightly tucked between mattress and frame, and drapes closed to keep the heat out.

Agatha used to wonder how strangers lived. Now, how those she knows justify how they live. Not what impels them to act.

She could encircle their home. Sit on the elevated porch. Tanuuj would follow but at a distance, both from her and the house. The dog and the man would not wait but leave. Yet this would only delay the inevitable.

Sometimes there is a lapse in disconnection. She believes the vigilantes know why she acts. Her movements question borders, property. They are never still but refuse to move for another body. They are barriers. Their inability to question why they curtail others' wills makes them incomprehensible.

By identifying their strangeness, she recognizes herself. Understands her motives for continuing the chase. This man may leave them alone. Later he or one like him will resume the chase. To keep walking is to confront what she cannot escape.

They reach the end of La Paz del Chaco. Where it does not turn onto the avenue but ends with a fence. Behind it lies a patch of yellow grass and trees with branches that curl with strain.

A horizontal, steel rod perforating vertical, wooden stakes. They bend in two, Tanuuj and Agatha. Fit between the pole and the floor. The way Tanuuj used to crawl under the branches of the thorn bushes by impelling his body with elbows and knees.

She hears the pat of paws against soil as hard as cement. Does not turn. Knows pet and owner follow. The sound lifts her out of her body. Not to see herself. She floats higher. To see the colony, settlement, and forest from above. Time advances.

People and animals distinguish themselves from things because they move. Even the cars or bicycles and cans are propelled by feet that kick and turn or push pedals. Streets that separate homes are lines drawn through movement too.

Smoke makes it hard to attach sound to source. It spreads across the sky, carried by the wind. She smells the stench of something burning. Things burnt to a crisp lift off the ground and evaporate into the air, filling her lungs.

The air is darkest a mile from the colony. Not in Cayim ô Clim, which starts north of La Guerra del Chaco Street. But west, following La Paz del Chaco to where it ends and continuing through the matted forest.

She imagines her little home ablaze. The arsonist would only have to rest a torch on the beams that hold the roof overhead. In the suffocating heat, the flames would spread and he would flee.

Her body moves towards the origin of the fire. The smell of smoke grows stronger. Floating out of her body to reach the height of a bird with the wingspan broad enough to see the three adjoining yet segregated zones at once is an illusion. The fire is real.

There is something odd, beyond fear, about her silence. Tanuuj knows Agatha sees something other than what lies before them. Her eyes are pinned to the *carancho*. It follows them from above. At the same distance from behind, Mark and his dog.

She sees the shack burned to ashes, the tree within aflame, a white horse where the door stood, and smoke spreading through the air, it keeps her in rapture for a while. She has never seemed more at peace than now, before impending violence.

He can still predict her movements. Knows her, not the future.

Knows she is not mad.

In slowness she builds the courage to face what will occur when the chase ceases. She looks further into the future, past the horror of foreshadowed violence which plays like a scene from a movie she barely performs in, at the stillness that will remain after the consummation of the act.

As her awareness grows heightened, she has something to gain in loss. She chooses not to flee the vision. She is driven by the desire to face something that will hang over her like this terrible black smoke until she extinguishes the source.

Tanuuj smells it too but knows only the stubble of the soy fields, which lie beyond the thorn forest that encircles their home, is ablaze. Agatha mistakes slash-and-burn agriculture for arson, the crops for the trees, and the forest for her home.

Out of fear that her body will be caught by nature, man, or beast she escapes in her mind.

There is logic to flight, if something is sought. She wants to see everything at once. With distance details dissolve so the thing before her merges with what is beside it and beside that, until a single plane appears.

Her own audible exhale, like a sigh, awakens her. It is sound and touch that frightens her most. The first foreshadows and the latter dissolves distance. Both make the thing proximate real.

Turning away from sight she wants to feel everything. Touch dissolves distance. Tracing the outline of the thing makes it real. You can feel the air when it is thick. It coats everything. Things lose their identity

Still some things never lose definition. She notices the *palo borracho* beside her. Its bloated gut is wider than any other. Its roots so deep they suck the moisture from a mile's circumference. These trees surpass the power of the Mennonite's irrigation system.

Agatha brings her hand to touch its trunk. It feels like a porcupine's pelt. The thorns do not pierce her flesh to make her bleed. They scratch her wet skin to ease the itch. Heal what the sun does to a woman this pale.

The heat forces the water from within to pour from her pores. She is left dry. Unlike the husky exterior of this trunk, which simulates dryness to keep the hummingbirds from piercing it the way they do the stigmas of its flowers.

Everything is surface. She cannot reach the inside of the tree because it is not hollow. Can only feel her own interior by picking her lips apart to caress her tongue and the roof of her mouth. Everything can be deeper.

The breeze envelops her the way the dirt buries the roots. They reach where soil gives way to water. The air fills rather than suffocates her. It reaches where touch cannot.

Things only own the space they occupy. Encircle the objects that protrude. Reach what is far: her home, the highway to the neighboring colony, the river that grows far from the badlands in the opposite direction. Lifts what is small: insects, leaves, blades of grass.

There, the tree, the ground, the fence. Behind her, the men. Beside her, the dog at her feet. They watch her constantly. Trying to understand what she cannot from within. Though nothing of what she thinks turns real. She simply remains still when she should move.

They want to know her from within. Understand what she thinks when she is silent. Why she moves with ease. What childhood event defined her as an adult. What part of her is unchanged.

The sun's heat and light are like the man's hands that transform soil or flesh, wringing them dry of water or life. She stops stroking the tree to look at their hands. One dark and the other reddened, both coarse. She can imagine them handling rope.

Without reaching out she can still feel where their flesh wrinkles. It is like leather. Once moistened, it dries with deep creases. She wonders if part of them is dead already because they cannot grow new life within.

They seek to fill me because they are empty, she thinks. Stops this thought. A shift occurs. A readiness for change, not provoked by cruelty, but the unnatural, supernatural.

She wants to transform into a sculpture. To become unfeeling like stone. To morph into what she is not. Midflight she ceases moving. Believing she will get caught. No one reaches out to grasp her. She does not mutate.

Everyone and everything mimics her stillness. Even the wind seems to drop to the ground as the pressure augments. No air. The sky turns dark. Agatha, Tanuuj, Mark, and the dog peer up. Clouds have appeared overhead. It rains.

Water falls so heavily it is audible. It soaks her clothes and hair. Everything touches her. Does not seek the core where roots perforate soil to reach an aquifer. Does not want to rise to heaven where clouds, planes, and birds are propelled by wind below. Everything—earth, water, air, fire—is material.

All that exists is expansion. The streets, avenues, and highways that delimit the inhabited from the uninhabitable are artificial. The invisible barrier around the colony and the visible one around her home can be trespassed.

Past and present converge because distance cannot collapse. She sees her mother again. Karin's clothes are as soaked as Agatha's. There is something ephemeral and compelling about moisture in a place where the sun dries everything in sight.

Karin

Karin's nearly lifeless body floats down the Pilcomayo. Hard, thick bones weighing down flesh. Thin, now translucent, cotton dress surfacing. Face turned to see the river floor. Hair stretching in every direction.

This still scene substitutes the glaring reality Agatha suppresses.

Arms and legs spread. Face upturned. Features bulging. Flesh turned blue around the gaping mouth and closed eyes. A weight carried within furrowed the brow and forced the lids shut.

A fight with oneself is visible in a drowned body. Karin died in the hospital, with assistance for breathing. The romantic image of submission does not do her justice. She was forced to desist, as was Verena.

The men that watched her, until they returned to work in the field and she walked into the river, betrayed her. They misunderstood her, obeyed. Her orders were questions. Their silent admiration for her endurance killed her.

She regained consciousness in the hospital. They asked her,

"Why?" She said her feet led her to the water. They said she was following the river to the sea. Protesting that the country is landlocked. She became a martyr, not a suicide, for the church and her family.

Karin was just seeking relief from the heat. It drives a woman this pale mad. All the men are. They work in the field, do not halt at midday, when the sun blazes like fire. Within her frigid home in ironed clothes standing by the double-pane window she watched bodies sweat.

It is this desire to endure that she sought to suspend by letting the water seep into her lungs instead of air. She wanted to stop knowing best. The instructions received from a hallucinated Christ weekly at mass were growing too difficult to carry out.

Her life led in the cool, empty space of a home was as tightly regimented as the grid that determined the street on which her home still stands. She entered the kitchen to prepare breakfast, each room to fix the beds, the bathroom to scrub the bath.

Her words reflected her actions and instructed others.

She wrote on the upper right corner of every page of her daughter's notebook, "Keep your back straight." Her own spine was as unbending as the columns that held the roof over their heads.

She whispered to her youngest son, "Notice his shortness of breath." He stopped running, so his older brother would not feel feeble.

Acted intentionally. When everything was done, she regained stillness. When nothing was left to say, she turned quiet.

When no one was around, she was alone.

Peering around the room she noticed the things she owned. She chose or inherited them. Despite her care they bear silent recriminations of use. Heat marks on the *quebracho* table, menstrual blood on the mattress, mold between the tiles.

She appeared untouchable during her wake.

Mother taught daughter to endure the school day without taking pleasure from the midday break. They were secretly admired. The relief Karin sought did not create a lapse in consciousness of time but ended her life.

Agatha should have been baptized in the Pilcomayo. The heat was unbearable that day. Cows and fish, not yet buried, rested on the dry riverbed. Children in white with their parents and the preacher knew it was an omen.

The third generation would not live like the second but the first.

Verena

Verena Harder arrived in 1947 to Puerto Casado with a fatherless daughter, Karin. Most Paraguayan women were also widows at the time, after the Chaco War and World War II.

The Mennonite men in Fernheim likened her to themselves. She continued proving her endurance by fighting their insinuations. They kept a distance until it collapsed, and violence ensued.

She remained in Fernheim for two years. Then, cofounded

Neuland, Frauendorf, a village of women without men.

The female Russian refugees moved from their Canadian relative's still humble homes to a palm island in the matted forest. It was the thorn bushes, not the canvas tents, that shielded them from the sandstorms and the sun's force.

Once apart, they were accepted. They ceased needing from others and instead began resisting, exploiting their surroundings. Refusing aid meant that they sought water further below ground during the dry season and when food was scarce, they ate even the leanest animal.

The men of the neighboring colonies, Menno and Fernheim, wondered if the women of Frauendorf had extracted this obstinacy from their bodies. It frightened them. To give something away unintentionally.

Those same men feared that their daughters and wives would mimic them. The way Karin's feeble son tried to run at the pace of the stronger one, until his mother or own body disciplined him.

The women of Neuland sought pleasure in everything. They sang while they worked. It was not a pastime. Silence was painfully ruptured by the delicate pitch of their tuned voices.

They lived within one structure, shared their food, and reared each other's children. Mothers acted like sisters. They slept in a pile, the way the boars do. Teenagers seemed not to outgrow the genderless interaction between infants.

The elder and younger—mother, sibling, and daughter or son—were offered equal respect. An adolescent nearing the childbearing age respected the will of the baby she cared for as she did his mother's autonomy. Every interaction, stripped of hierarchy, between people.

The intention behind acting was always only to gain communal strength. Life was joyful though streaked with pain. Their daughters learned the difference between means and ends from their adoptive fathers. They sacrificed pleasure for duty.

When the stray men arrived, they grew conscious of touch. They traveled from the closed labor camps to be reunited with their families. If the women they sought were declared dead, the surviving men found substitutes.

Peter worked harder than Verena. Made the fields bear fruit. Helped build a barn, a mill, and a school. Yet it was his wife that built their home. She arrived and settled before him. Her commitment allowed him to ease into her deceased spouse's place.

Viola's birth purged the ghost of Karin's birth father. She brought Peter, Verena, and Karin together. Then, tore them apart.

Their home was the one Agatha inhabits now. There is an openness to the feeble architecture that allows air to seep through the netted, floor to ceiling, windows in the front and back of the home, creating a current. She planted the tree her granddaughter prunes though it still pushes against the roof.

It was a house passersby could enter. Most slept on the veranda as Tanuuj does now. Some preferred to be indoors when it rained. None feared they would feel as unnatural as a pet. Now the sole female proprietor allows no one in.

Her grandmother died on a cloth on the floor like a drying leaf. She was not anesthetized when her hallucinations grew so real she became silent and still. Her expression changed. What she saw made her fear the people and animals that became other things.

She only described a vision once. Her daughters sat at her feet. She saw a man with eyes so black, the pupils and irises merged. He led her to the summit of a hill covered in squares of grass. Then, sat on the tortured protruding root of an *ombú*. She sat on his lap. He smiled. His teeth were stained. She had never seen anyone more beautiful.

The rest of her specters died with the memory of the senile woman. When Agatha cannot sleep she wonders if the specters she has met in places real or imagined have impregnated the walls of her bedroom with an odor that will inspire her dreams.

A hallucination is not sensed through sight, hearing, or touch, when it begins. It is smelled.

Before the scent of burning flesh reaches Agatha, something occurs. The rain stops. A horse appears from behind the *palo borracho*. His pelt quivers to frighten away mosquitos. The rain drips off his long, white hair. The unexpected brings her back into herself.

She feels him move through sight. He paces. Pauses. Faces her. She does not meet the stallion's gaze.

He has a large body. Occupies his place. Moving, displaces space. Intercepts the sun and the soil. A shadow grows from his hoofs. An extension and distorted rendition of a horse. He is undeniably present yet is more than what can be touched or observed.

His feet are planted in the soil. The rain can coat his pelt. The water can evaporate into the air. The other animals, things, and plants occupy other places he cannot fill. Instead of moving them, he acknowledges how they limit his movement through space.

She realizes what the men that watch her see. Glazing over her gaze makes her an impenetrable surface. Something inanimate that does not respond to speech or action. Does not bleed, if penetrated.

Her sense of belonging does not come from being recognized by those that live in the colony and surroundings. Instead, from her knowledge of the autochthonous flora. She can tell the poisonous plants from the edible, name the species, and guess their effects on a human body if ingested or touched.

Where the threads of the web of life meet, she can still tell things apart. It means that she is only herself in unison with her surroundings. The question is only whether she is at peace here.

Her grandmother fled the colony where she would be cared for in order to care for herself. Her home apart, was occupied by four. Other edifices rose around it. Then, the ground was found to be fertile. They were demolished and rebuilt close by, but where the land was barren.

Only the first house of Neuland and a portion of the surrounding forest remains intact. Her mother was born elsewhere, raised here, and educated in the capital only in order to be imprisoned in an empty home. Agatha finds herself in the same state but more vulnerable.

Karin sought the absent presence of things in death; Agatha, in madness. The desire to abandon the body stems from being enchained to the land they live on, where they belong. The contradiction lies in those who force them to stay. They fear what they do not know.

"There is no inside," she says. Tanuuj reaches out to touch her shoulder. The way Mark should have whistled to the dog. How she will stroke the horse's mane. Agatha pulls away. Disillusioned by touch. She wants to inhabit the future.

Catapults her body forth by interacting with what is not there yet. The stallion before her. She strokes his muzzle. Rests her torso against his. Weaves her arms around his neck. Lets her weight hang from his sturdy body. Swings one leg over his back. Mounts him. Gallops home.

The men behind her remain standing. Seeing what has escaped their grasp. What continues to move out of sight. They know where she is heading. Do not follow. Tanuuj sits at the foot of the *palo borracho*. Mark starts back down the road of churning soil and sand. Followed by his pet.

Agatha rides through the matted forest. The thorns pull at the horse's legs. He lifts them out from the woven branches. Making room for himself with force. She shields her face from the bowing branches of taller trees by burying it in the animal's pelt.

She has blinded herself. Caresses the tough, long hairs with her lashes. There is nothing beautiful about this escape. It is forceful. Still there is hope in becoming unrecognizable to oneself. An other is proximate elsewhere.

The wind subsides when the horse halts. Her knees press against his torso. He recognizes her home. He entered nine years ago. At nine years old Agatha realized no one would mind if she lived there. Six years have passed since she moved in at twelve. It is 2022 and she is eighteen.

A Home

In the summer of 2013, the heat grew more unbearable than ever before and they found petroleum in the groundwater. The Klassen clan would be rich. Survive on rainwater. Their livestock would die. Easy deaths.

The shack was emptied. The bed, chair, and wardrobe looked strange on the lawn. The animals, larger indoors. Her father bottle-fed water pumped from the ground to the zebus. There was cruelty in his empathy. They lay panting until still.

The house originally doubled as a barn. Verena and Karin had shared it with their mare. The roof and doorframe were built high enough to fit a horse.

At the foot of a threshold a copper plate: "Easier for a camel to fit through the eye of a needle than for a rich man to enter through the gates of heaven."

The first generation fought to stay. The third, to leave.

Agatha unmounts. Feels small and heavy at the same time. Returning to her unaltered size she is harmless. A willing or enslaved animal. Only with a gun could she become a threat. Everything looks the same. It should not.

She imagines abandoning her home. The tree's stiff branches would break through the roof and walls. The floor would splinter and mix with earth as the roots protrude from the soil. Birds would hide among the roof tiles and rodents, under the floorboards.

It would all come tumbling down with the perseverance of the wind and rain. She wonders about her heirlooms tucked in drawers, lets them go. Even the remnants of brick and glass would disappear into the hard ground like a buried body. The land was unforgiving that way.

Indifference towards the home begins when undomesticated animals are allowed indoors. Free to procreate, come and go. First, insects; then, rodents, birds, reptiles; once large mammals enter, it becomes a house taken over.

She leaves the door open. The stud follows her. She does not turn to watch him bend his head like a very tall man. His lush, white tail flicks and hits the frame. Treads carefully between wall and chair tucked into the table frame.

His ability to do what men cannot is spurred by her love for him. Some things are simpler for animals. He desires nothing more than to lie by her still body. The structure of her home allows both to fit under one roof.

Comprehension transcends words. First, he was a body conscious of her watching him move. Before distance elapsed between them something became intangibly understood. A mutual desire for proximity, not touch.

Contact began when she mounted him. This had occurred to her once before by force. Where her once flat stomach now protrudes is a reminder.

The sound of his hoofs, like hammers, against the wood, halts before the threshold.

The division between internal and external is transcended. The stud is like the heat of the sun or the movement of the wind. A force that does not obey the rules of men.

Nothing has ever been so beautifully out of place. The tree seems to stand more erect. It holds its place beside the beast. The walls are frailer. The cement between each carefully placed stone crumbles with each exhalation.

Agatha can see between the bricks. The dimming light outside. The long approaching shadow of a man. It crawls into itself as he slides down with his back against the wall to crouch by his feet. She can hear his recognizable steadiness of breath.

The rope still hangs from the back door. She loosens the knot and slips it off the knob. *It is strong*, she thinks. Taut if pulled from opposite ends. She can change the shape of things. Force them to stretch, bend, or break, like her body. Allow them to fall into their natural form.

She kneels beside the stud. With her left hand, caresses the knee of his right, front leg. It loosens. With her right, lifts his hoof. Slips it through the hole in the knot. Drapes the rope under his torso. Weaves it between his hind legs. Pulls softly. Uses the weight of her body to alter his posture.

His right front leg bends. Forearm reaches the floor. He does the rest on his own. The front left and hind legs fold to match. The entire body lowers. He lies flat. Succumbed to her will. He sleeps standing. Lying, he resembles himself, if dead.

From above he seems as inoffensive as a hen. His limbs do not curve this way naturally. She knows his joints will hurt when he rises back to full height. He rode her here, faster than her feet could carry, so she could tower over him.

For the first time in her life she does not want the day to end. Her relentless resilience subsides. She wants to rest without sleeping. She lies down at the foot of the tree. Her head atop the mound of soil that seeped between and over the floorboards.

With her ear to the earth she hears a stream running below.

Imagines the river her mother drowned in, now a dry bed, flowing again. The floating body resuscitating. Lulled awake by the easy movement of the water. A few strokes of her arms. Pushes her palms against the riverbank. Her body emerges. Dries on a patch of grass.

Opens her eyes. Sees the wall-enclosed tree is not forcing open the roof but its tortured branches are longing to extend. Meets the gaze of the woken horse and sees in him something beyond the glistening pupils, a plea. A distance grows between her and those she makes bend.

She is intolerant. They are resilient. Trees were uprooted to make room for her home. The space their roots occupied remains like a phantom hand reaching for the water further below that dries as it reaches.

Everything is alive, she realizes as she falls asleep.

Agatha dreams. Feels the white horse kick. He is drowning in the body of water she carries within. Pushed to the shore by the current. He climbs out. Age reverses. He is a foal. Long legs buckle. Insisting, gain traction. Gallops far. Out of sight.

Another kick and another. Now commanded by stiffer limbs. It is her mother paddling in the water. Instead of sinking to the riverbed she is swimming. The living carry an alternate reality in which the dead survive what killed them.

She feels them. The one doing the kicking is not visible. She is elsewhere. Transported to a bed. Her legs propped on stirrups.

Pain bends her. Force separates her from what grows within. The head presses where her body opens. Like her own against the headboard when she feared men.

Her own clenched body tears and softens. The foreign body that came out of her own releases a cry. First, it sounds like a wounded animal. She recognizes the sound before she sees her. It is instant. Her daughter.

Estela is by her side. Even her hands are lush. They are interlocked with her own bony fingers. She lies, "Nothing will happen to her." Someone places the cotton bundle in her arms. It is warm. She feels the child's cheek with the back of her hand.

Her face is mesmerizing. Eyes such a light shade of blue that they are nearly transparent. She does not see through Agatha, but Agatha sees through her. Like gazing at the sea. It appears blue. Then, translucent. You could see the ocean floor if the salt did not get in your eyes.

Thick, white eyebrows that curve at the ends but join in the middle frame her gaze. She looks like a bird. A white hue to her feathers. Not a pigeon, a dove. She is older for an instant. Agatha sees her perched on a branch of the *ombú* in the middle of their home. So, they remain?

Her gaze is never fixed on the thing before her. It floats up to meet what flies above her. The ceiling—cracks or textured cement, between the branches of the tree—the sun splintering apart the leaves, an airplane tracing a white line in the sky simply with its speed.

Her mouth is small. Lips curl up and indent at the center like the knot in a bow. Once she outgrows breastmilk, the food she is fed must be placed a morsel at a time on that tiny tongue. Her mother wonders if her own hands are too large to feed such a delicate being.

She is heavier than a bird. You can tell by the size of her hands and feet that she will be tall. She will speak softly. She will play harder than other girls. The hardness of her bones foretells that she will fight back, if pinned down.

Hair so light and thick you cannot see her scalp. Once she grows old enough to walk, it coats her back and reaches her bum. It is as white as snow at dawn before it is trampled. She sweats below the heavy mane but never fastens it.

She will refuse to cut it. Throw herself on the floor with the rage of white heat. Something terrible will happen if her mother trims the ends. It is a part of her. She strokes it to fall asleep at night. It adorns her in daylight.

Her name is Concepción. It means conception. Agatha refuses not to name the father. The day she was born it rained *lapacho* flowers. If an animal can care for a woman, the earth, wind, water, and fire can pity their child.

Concepción

Acknowledgments

Versions of the stories in the "Cayim ô Clim" section were published by *RIC, Entropy,* and *SLUG.* I thank the editors of those publications for their generous encouragement, and for expanding my ideas of fiction and place.

── ABOUT THE AUTHOR ──

Elisa Taber is a writer, translator, and anthropologist. Her writing and translations are troubled into being, even when that trouble is a kind of joy. She edits *SLUG* and an Amerindian poetry series for *Words without Borders*. Elisa lives between Buenos Aires and Montreal, where she is writing a PhD at McGill University on the ontological poetics of Amerindian literature.